Table of Contents

Chapter 1: Introduction to Google Bard 27
   1.1 The Rise of AI in Search Technology 27
   1.2 Understanding Google Bard's Capabilities 28
      1. Natural Language Understanding 28
      2. Personalization 28
      3. Voice Search 29
      4. Semantic Search 29
      5. Conversational AI 29
      6. Multimodal Search 29
      7. Real-time Updates 30
      8. Complex Query Handling 30
      9. Integration with Other Google Services 30
   1.3 The Evolution from Traditional Search Engines to AI-Powered Solutions 30
      1. Traditional Keyword-Based Search Engines 31
      2. The Rise of Semantic Search 31
      3. Machine Learning and Natural Language Processing 31
      4. Personalization and User Insights 32
      5. Conversational AI and Voice Search 32
      6. Multimodal Search and Rich Content 32
      7. Real-time Updates and Alerts 32
      8. Integration with Ecosystem 32
      9. Continuous Advancements 33
   1.4 Navigating the Interface of Google Bard 33
      1. Search Bar and Query Input 33
      2. Search Results 34
      3. Filters and Advanced Search Options 34

4. Voice Search and Assistant 34

5. Recommendations and Suggestions 34

6. Conversation History 35

7. User Profile and Settings 35

8. Real-time Updates and Alerts 35

9. Integration with Other Services 35

1.5 Setting Expectations: What Google Bard Can and Cannot Do 36

What Google Bard Can Do 36

What Google Bard Cannot Do 37

Chapter 2: Getting Started with Google Bard 39

2.1 Creating a Google Bard Account 39

1. Accessing the Registration Page 39

2. Providing Your Information 39

3. Verification and Authentication 40

4. Setting Up Your Profile 40

5. Customizing Preferences 40

6. Exploring the Interface 40

7. Learning Basic Search Techniques 41

2.2 Customizing Your User Experience 41

1. Personalizing Your Profile 41

2. Language and Region Preferences 42

3. Search History and Personalization 42

4. Customizing the Home Page 42

5. Privacy Settings 43

6. Notifications and Alerts 43

7. Theme and Appearance 43

2.3 Basic and Advanced Search Techniques 44

    1. Basic Keyword Search 44

    2. Exact Phrase Search 45

    3. Boolean Operators 45

    4. Site-Specific Search 45

    5. File Type Search 45

    6. Advanced Query Operators 46

    7. Advanced Filters 46

    8. Voice Search 46

    9. Conversational Search 46

    10. Multimodal Search 47

2.4 Interpreting Google Bard's Responses 47

    1. Result Structure 47

    2. Relevance Ranking 48

    3. Click-Through Behavior 48

    4. Evaluating Snippets 48

    5. Refining Queries 48

    6. Voice Responses 49

    7. Conversation History 49

    8. Multimodal Content 49

    9. Real-Time Updates 50

    10. Verification of Information 50

2.5 Tips for Efficient Information Retrieval 50

    1. Use Descriptive Keywords 51

    2. Refine Your Query 51

    3. Utilize Advanced Search Operators 51

    4. Check Related Searches 51

    5. Explore Advanced Filters 52

    6. Use Voice Search for Convenience 52

- 7. Maintain a Search History 52
- 8. Bookmark Important Sources 52
- 9. Stay Informed About Updates 53
- 10. Cross-Verify Critical Information 53

Chapter 3: Advanced Features and Tools 54

- 3.1 Utilizing Voice Search with Google Bard 54
  - 1. Activating Voice Search 54
  - 2. Speaking Clearly and Concisely 54
  - 3. Natural Language Queries 54
  - 4. Voice Commands 55
  - 5. Voice Search for Accessibility 55
  - 6. Supported Languages 55
  - 7. Voice Response Feedback 55
  - 8. Privacy Considerations 56
  - 9. Troubleshooting Voice Recognition 56
  - 10. Feedback and Improvements 56
- 3.2 Exploring Bard's Interactive Elements 57
  - 1. Interactive Cards 57
  - 2. Knowledge Panels 57
  - 3. Featured Snippets 57
  - 4. Interactive Maps 58
  - 5. Carousel Browsing 58
  - 6. In-SERP Actions 58
  - 7. Instant Answers 58
  - 8. Visual Search 59
  - 9. Conversational Search 59
  - 10. Real-Time Updates 59
- 3.3 Advanced Query Formulation 60

1. Exact Match 60

2. Boolean Operators 60

3. Site-Specific Searches 60

4. File Type Searches 61

5. Related Keywords 61

6. Exclude Terms 61

7. Wildcard Searches 61

8. Range Searches 61

9. Intitle and Inurl Operators 62

10. Date Filters 62

3.4 Personalization and Privacy Settings 62

1. Personalized Search Results 63

2. Location-Based Results 63

3. Search History Management 63

4. Ad Personalization 63

5. SafeSearch Filters 64

6. Incognito Mode 64

7. Data Retention and Deletion 64

8. Privacy Controls 64

9. Account Security 65

10. Consent for Data Usage 65

3.5 Integrating Google Bard with Other Google Services 65

1. Google Account Integration 66

2. Google Drive Integration 66

3. Google Calendar Integration 66

4. Google Maps Integration 66

5. Google Photos Integration 66

6. Google Translate Integration 67

- 7. YouTube Integration 67
- 8. Google Assistant Integration.....................................67
- 9. Google Workspace Integration 67
- 10. Voice Commands for Integration 68

Chapter 4: Google Bard in Everyday Life 69
4.1 Enhancing Personal Productivity 69
- 1. Task Management 69
- 2. Calendar Integration 69
- 3. Note-taking and Documentation..............................69
- 4. Email Management 70
- 5. Language Translation 70
- 6. Setting Reminders 70
- 7. News and Updates...70
- 8. Time Management...70
- 9. Health and Fitness 71
- 10. Productivity Tracking 71

4.2 Using Google Bard for Educational Purposes 71
- 1. Research Assistance 72
- 2. Study Aid 72
- 3. Language Learning...72
- 4. Access to Educational Resources 72
- 5. Math and Science Support 73
- 6. Citation and References 73
- 7. Historical and Cultural Information 73
- 8. Encouraging Critical Thinking 73
- 9. Interactive Learning 73
- 10. Collaborative Learning 74

4.3 Shopping and Consumer Research...........................74

- 1. Product Research 74
- 2. Price Comparison 75
- 3. User Reviews 75
- 4. Discounts and Deals 75
- 5. Shopping Lists 75
- 6. Local Shopping 75
- 7. Product Recommendations 76
- 8. Delivery Tracking 76
- 9. Return and Warranty Information 76
- 10. Product Availability 76

4.4 Travel Planning and Local Information 77
- 1. Trip Planning 77
- 2. Flight and Hotel Reservations 77
- 3. Local Attractions 77
- 4. Dining Recommendations 78
- 5. Public Transportation 78
- 6. Weather Updates 78
- 7. Currency Conversion 78
- 8. Language Assistance 79
- 9. Local Events and Entertainment 79
- 10. Emergency Information 79

4.5 Entertainment and Media Queries 80
- 1. Movie and TV Show Information 80
- 2. Music Exploration 80
- 3. Book Recommendations 80
- 4. Gaming Information 81
- 5. Sports Updates 81
- 6. Event Tickets 81

7. News and Celebrity Gossip 81
8. Movie and Music Recommendations 81
9. Gaming Tips and Strategies 82
10. Media Streaming 82
Chapter 5: Business Applications of Google Bard 83
5.1 Market Research and Data Analysis 83
1. Competitive Analysis 83
2. Industry Trends and Insights 83
3. Customer Feedback Analysis 83
4. Data Visualization 84
5. Market Surveys and Research 84
6. Pricing Strategy 84
7. Sales Forecasting 84
8. Product Development Insights 85
9. Brand Reputation Monitoring 85
10. Investment and Market Entry Analysis 85
5.2 Enhancing SEO and Digital Marketing 86
1. Keyword Research 86
2. Content Optimization 86
3. Backlink Analysis 86
4. Competitor Analysis 87
5. SEO Audits 87
6. Local SEO 87
7. Content Marketing Ideas 87
8. Social Media Strategies 88
9. Paid Advertising Guidance 88
10. Performance Tracking 88
5.3 Customer Service and Engagement 89

- 1. Instant Customer Support 89
- 2. FAQ Automation 89
- 3. Product Recommendations 89
- 4. Order Status Updates 89
- 5. Troubleshooting Assistance 90
- 6. Appointment Scheduling 90
- 7. Feedback Collection 90
- 8. Product Knowledge Base 90
- 9. Loyalty Programs and Rewards 91
- 10. Follow-Up and Surveys 91

5.4 Competitive Analysis 91
- 1. Competitor Identification 92
- 2. SWOT Analysis 92
- 3. Market Share and Positioning 92
- 4. Product and Service Offerings 92
- 5. Pricing Strategies 93
- 6. Customer Reviews and Feedback 93
- 7. Marketing and Advertising Analysis 93
- 8. Innovation and Research 93
- 9. Online Presence and SEO 94
- 10. Benchmarking and Strategy Development 94

5.5 Trends Forecasting and Industry Insights 94
- 1. Trend Analysis 95
- 2. Consumer Behavior Insights 95
- 3. Market Research Reports 95
- 4. Technology Trends 95
- 5. Competitive Intelligence 96
- 6. Regulatory Changes 96

7. Global Market Insights...96
8. Industry Events and Conferences..96
9. Investment Opportunities..97
10. Predictive Analytics 97

Chapter 6: Understanding AI and Natural Language Processing 98

6.1 The Basics of AI in Search Engines..98
   1. What is Artificial Intelligence? 98
   2. The Role of AI in Search Engines..98
   3. Machine Learning and Search Ranking....................................99
   4. Natural Language Processing (NLP)...99
   5. Conversational AI 99
   6. AI in Understanding User Intent 99
   7. Future Possibilities with AI 100

6.2 How Google Bard Processes Language 100
   1. Text Tokenization 100
   2. Part-of-Speech Tagging 101
   3. Named Entity Recognition (NER) 101
   4. Dependency Parsing...101
   5. Sentiment Analysis...101
   6. Language Translation...102
   7. Question Answering...102
   8. Contextual Understanding 102
   9. Multilingual Support...102
   10. Continuous Learning..103

6.3 The Role of Machine Learning 103
   1. Training Data 103
   2. Natural Language Understanding..103

    3. Personalization 104
    4. Search Ranking 104
    5. User Intent Prediction 104
    6. Contextual Understanding 104
    7. Continuous Improvement 105
    8. Data Privacy 105
    9. Multilingual Capabilities 105
    10. Future Developments 105
6.4 AI Ethics and Responsible Use 106
    1. Fairness and Bias Mitigation 106
    2. Transparency 106
    3. Privacy by Design 106
    4. User Consent 107
    5. Data Security 107
    6. Accountability and Governance 107
    7. Addressing Ethical Dilemmas 107
    8. User Education 108
    9. Continuous Monitoring and Improvement 108
    10. Ethical AI Community 108
6.5 Limitations and Challenges of AI in Search 109
    1. Data Dependence 109
    2. Biased Training Data 109
    3. Ethical Dilemmas 109
    4. Contextual Understanding 110
    5. Personalization Balance 110
    6. Scalability 110
    7. User Privacy 110
    8. Misinformation and Disinformation 111

- 9. User Interface Design 111
- 10. Evolving Technology 111

Chapter 7: Google Bard for Content Creators 112

7.1 Researching and Generating Ideas 112
- 1. Comprehensive Information Retrieval 112
- 2. Trend Analysis 112
- 3. Exploring Niche Topics 112
- 4. Competitive Analysis 113
- 5. Idea Generation Techniques 113
- 6. Data Visualization Tools 113
- 7. Content Validation 113
- 8. Collaboration and Sharing 114
- 9. Ethical Content Creation 114
- 10. Continuous Learning 114

7.2 Analyzing Audience Trends 115
- 1. Audience Segmentation 115
- 2. Content Engagement Metrics 115
- 3. Keyword Analysis 115
- 4. Social Media Monitoring 116
- 5. Audience Surveys and Feedback 116
- 6. Competitive Analysis 116
- 7. Content Personalization 116
- 8. Content Testing 117
- 9. Feedback Integration 117
- 10. Content Evolution 117

7.3 SEO Optimization for Content 118
- 1. Keyword Research 118
- 2. On-Page SEO 118

- 3. Content Quality and Relevance 119
- 4. Backlink Building 119
- 5. Mobile Optimization 119
- 6. Page Speed Optimization 119
- 7. SEO Plugins and Tools 120
- 8. Schema Markup 120
- 9. SEO Analytics 120
- 10. SEO Best Practices 120

7.4 Monitoring Content Performance 121
- 1. Website Analytics 121
- 2. Social Media Insights 121
- 3. Email Campaign Analytics 122
- 4. Content A/B Testing 122
- 5. Conversion Tracking 122
- 6. Heatmaps and User Behavior Analysis 123
- 7. SEO Performance Metrics 123
- 8. Content Engagement Metrics 123
- 9. Performance Reports 123
- 10. Continuous Improvement 124

7.5 Collaborating and Sharing Insights 124
- 1. Shared Document and Workspace 125
- 2. Comment and Feedback System 125
- 3. Version Control 125
- 4. Task Assignment and Management 125
- 5. Integration with Project Management Tools 126
- 6. Reporting and Insights Sharing 126
- 7. Content Calendar Collaboration 126
- 8. Meeting Integration 127

- 9. Knowledge Sharing 127
- 10. Security and Access Control 127
- 8.1 Addressing Search Accuracy Problems 128
  - 1. Query Refinement 128
  - 2. Filtering and Sorting 128
  - 3. Semantic Search 129
  - 4. Utilizing Advanced Search Operators 129
  - 5. Feedback Mechanism 129
  - 6. Continuous Learning 130
  - 7. Accessibility and User Assistance 130
- 8.2 Handling Misunderstandings and Errors 130
  - 1. Query Clarification 131
  - 2. Error Messages and Suggestions 131
  - 3. Search Query History 131
  - 4. User Feedback Loop 132
  - 5. Contextual Understanding 132
  - 6. User Assistance and Tutorials 132
  - 7. Continuous Improvement 132
- 8.3 Updating User Preferences and Settings 133
  - 1. Personalization 133
  - 2. Privacy Settings 134
  - 3. Notifications and Alerts 134
  - 4. Accessibility Options 134
  - 5. Search Results Display 134
  - 6. Help and Support 135
  - 7. Consistent User Profile 135
  - 8. Default Settings 135
  - 9. User Education 136

8.4 Reporting Bugs and Providing Feedback.................................136
   1. Importance of User Feedback..136
   2. User-Friendly Feedback Mechanisms 137
   3. Clear Reporting Process...137
   4. Bug Reporting Form 137
   5. Anonymous Reporting Option..137
   6. Response Time 137
   7. Categorization and Prioritization 137
   8. Regular Bug Fix Releases 138
   9. User Communication 138
   10. Feedback Analysis 138
   11. Feedback Integration...138
   12. Feedback Loop...138
   13. User Incentives..138
   14. User Education 138
8.5 Staying Informed About Updates and Changes....................139
   1. Release Notes...139
   2. In-App Notifications...139
   3. Email Updates..140
   4. Blog or News Section 140
   5. Social Media Channels...140
   6. Webinars and Tutorials..140
   7. User Community Forums...140
   8. Feedback and Suggestions 140
   9. Regular Newsletters 141
   10. Customer Support..141
   11. Transparency 141
   12. User Surveys..141

13. Update Frequency 141
14. Beta Testing Programs 141
15. Accessibility 142
9.1 Understanding Data Collection and Use 143
  Data Collection Principles 143
  Types of Data Collected 143
    1. Search Queries 143
    2. Location Information 144
    3. Usage Statistics 144
    4. Device Information 144
    5. Personalization Data 144
    6. Cookies and Tracking 144
  Data Usage 144
    1. Improving Search Quality 144
    2. Personalization 144
    3. Analytics 145
    4. Ad Targeting 145
  Privacy Settings 145
  Security Measures 145
  User Responsibility 145
  Managing Your Digital Footprint 146
    Why Manage Your Digital Footprint? 146
    Tips for Managing Your Digital Footprint 147
    Conclusion 148
  Security Features and Protocols 148
    1. Encryption 149
    2. Virtual Private Networks (VPNs) 149
    3. Two-Factor Authentication (2FA) 149

4. Strong Password Practices 150
5. Security Updates and Patching 150
6. Firewalls 150
7. Secure Browsing Practices 150
8. Data Backups 151
9. Online Shopping and Financial Transactions 151
10. Security Awareness and Education 151
Conclusion 152
Best Practices for Protecting Personal Information 152
1. Data Minimization 152
2. Privacy Settings 152
3. Secure Wi-Fi Networks 153
4. Phishing Awareness 153
5. Password Hygiene 153
6. Multi-Factor Authentication (MFA) 154
7. Regularly Monitor Accounts 154
8. App Permissions 154
9. Secure File Storage 154
10. Keep Software Updated 155
Conclusion 155
The Future of Privacy in AI-Powered Search 155
1. Enhanced Privacy Controls 155
2. Differential Privacy 156
3. Federated Learning 156
4. Blockchain for Data Control 156
5. Ethical AI and Transparency 157
6. Legislation and Regulation 157
7. Privacy-Centric Search Engines 157

- 8. User Education ... 158
- 9. Privacy-Enhancing Technologies ... 158
- 10. Collaborative Efforts ... 158
- Conclusion ... 158

Incorporating Bard into Classroom Learning ... 160
- 1. Personalized Learning ... 160
  - Example: Research Projects ... 160
- 2. Facilitating Discussion ... 160
  - Example: Current Events ... 160
- 3. Supporting Homework and Assignments ... 161
  - Example: Essay Writing ... 161
- 4. Encouraging Digital Literacy ... 161
  - Example: Search Strategy Workshops ... 161
- 5. Preparing for Research Projects ... 161
  - Example: Research Workshops ... 161
- 6. Collaborative Learning ... 162
  - Example: Group Projects ... 162
- 7. Assessment and Evaluation ... 162
  - Example: Research Portfolios ... 162
- 8. Accessibility and Inclusivity ... 162
  - Example: Audiobooks and Summaries ... 162
- Conclusion ... 162

Facilitating Research and Study ... 163
- 1. Comprehensive Information Retrieval ... 163
- 2. Efficient Literature Reviews ... 163
- 3. Organizing Research Materials ... 164
- 4. Advanced Search Techniques ... 164
  - Example: Advanced Query ... 164

- 5. Citation Management 164
- 6. Collaborative Research 164
- 7. Staying Informed 165
- 8. Enhancing Critical Thinking 165
- Example: Evaluating Sources 165
- 9. Access to Diverse Formats 165
- 10. Preparing for Exams 165
- Conclusion 166

Encouraging Critical Thinking and Analysis 166
- 1. Diverse Sources of Information 166
- 2. Evaluating Source Credibility 166
- 3. Analyzing and Synthesizing Information 167
- 4. Questioning and Inquiry 167
- Example: Inquiry-Based Learning 167
- 5. Fact-Checking and Debunking Misinformation 167
- 6. Ethical Considerations 167
- 7. Problem-Solving Skills 168
- 8. Encouraging Discussion and Debate 168
- 9. Lifelong Learning 168
- Conclusion 168

Balancing Technology and Traditional Learning Methods 169
- 1. Enhancing Traditional Teaching 169
- 2. Supporting Personalized Learning 169
- 3. Fostering Collaborative Learning 169
- 4. Bridging Gaps in Access to Information 170
- 5. Preparing Students for the Digital Age 170
- 6. Addressing Challenges and Concerns 170
- 7. Professional Development for Educators 170

- 8. Encouraging a Growth Mindset 170
- 9. Measuring the Impact 171
- 10. Continuous Improvement 171
- Conclusion 171

Preparing Students for an AI-Driven World 171
- 1. AI Literacy and Awareness 172
- 2. Integrating AI into the Curriculum 172
- 3. Problem-Solving and Critical Thinking 173
- 4. Ethical AI Use 173
- 5. Collaboration and Interdisciplinary Learning 173
- 6. Lifelong Learning Mindset 173
- 7. Real-World Applications 173
- 8. Soft Skills and Adaptability 174
- 9. Encouraging Innovation 174
- 10. Collaboration with AI Industry 174

Chapter 11: Social and Cultural Impacts 178
- 11.1 Google Bard's Influence on Information Consumption 178

11.2 Bridging Cultural and Language Barriers 180
11.3 The Role in Promoting Digital Literacy 182
11.4 Addressing Misinformation and Bias 184
11.5 Fostering Global Knowledge Exchange 186
12.1 Current Trends and Innovations 189
12.2 Predicting the Next Steps for Google Bard 192
12.3 The Role of User Feedback in Shaping AI 195
- The Feedback Loop 195
- Types of User Feedback 196
- The Evolution of AI Systems 196

User-Centric Development 197
12.4 Ethical Considerations and Future Challenges 198
Transparency and Explainability 198
Bias and Fairness 198
Privacy and Data Protection 198
Algorithmic Accountability 199
Socioeconomic Impact 199
Environmental Sustainability 199
International Regulations and Governance 199
Ethical User Education 199
Future Challenges and Collaborative Solutions 200
12.5 Imagining the Long-Term Impact of AI on Information Access 200
Enhanced Information Retrieval 200
Personalization and Hyper-Personalization 200
AI-Augmented Creativity 201
Ethical and Bias-Free AI 201
AI-Powered Education 201
Global Access to Information 201
Sustainable AI 201
Human-AI Collaboration 202
AI Ethics and Governance 202
Continuous Learning and Adaptation 202
13.1 Crafting Precise Search Queries 202
Understanding the Basics 203
Specificity Matters 203
Boolean Logic for Precision 204
Advanced Query Techniques 204

13.2 Utilizing Filters and Advanced Search Options 205
    The Power of Filters 205
    Advanced Search Operators 206
    Using Filters and Advanced Options Effectively 207
13.3 Deciphering and Evaluating Search Results 208
    Understanding Search Snippets 208
    Evaluating Relevance and Credibility 208
    Clicking and Exploring 209
    Using Advanced Search Features 209
    Honing Your Evaluation Skills 210
13.4 Leveraging Google Bard for Complex Queries 210
    Boolean Operators 210
    Phrase Searching 211
    Site and Domain-Specific Searches 211
    Advanced Search Filters 211
    Using Wildcards 211
    Exploring Related Searches 212
    Combining Techniques 212
13.5 Continuous Learning and Adaptation 212
    Staying Informed 212
    Experimentation and Adaptation 213
    Lifelong Learning 214
14.1 Connecting with Other Google Bard Users 215
    Joining Online Forums and Communities 215
    Benefits of Community Engagement 215
    Tips for Effective Engagement 216
14.2 Participating in Forums and Discussion Groups 217
    Benefits of Forum Participation 217

    Finding the Right Forums 217

    Tips for Effective Participation 218

  14.3 Sharing Tips and Best Practices 219

    Why Share Tips and Best Practices? 219

    Effective Tip Sharing 220

    Best Practices for Contribution 220

    Encouraging Discussion 221

  14.4 Collaborative Learning and Support 222

    The Power of Collaborative Learning 222

    Effective Collaboration and Support 222

    Building a Supportive Community 224

  14.5 Building a Community of Informed Users 225

    The Significance of Informed User Communities 225

    Tips for Building and Nurturing Informed User Communities 226

Chapter 15: Personal Development and Learning 229

  15.1 Using Google Bard for Self-Improvement 229

    Self-Improvement and Lifelong Learning 229

    Practical Tips for Self-Improvement with Google Bard 230

  15.2 Lifelong Learning and Skill Development 232

    The Importance of Lifelong Learning 232

    Google Bard as a Lifelong Learning Tool 233

    Strategies for Effective Lifelong Learning 234

  15.3 Exploring Diverse Topics and Interests 235

    The Significance of Exploring Diverse Topics 235

    Leveraging Google Bard for Diverse Exploration 236

    Tips for Effective Exploration 237

  15.4 Staying Informed and Curious 238

The Significance of Curiosity 239
Nurturing Curiosity 239
Google Bard as a Curiosity Companion 240
Practical Tips for Staying Curious 241
15.5 Balancing Technology with Personal Growth 242
The Digital Age Dilemma 242
Strategies for Balancing Technology and Personal Growth
.... 243
Google Bard as an Ally in Balance 244
Conclusion 245
Chapter 16: Google Bard in Creative Industries 246
Section 16.1: Assisting Writers and Journalists 246
Enhancing Research Efforts 246
Improving Writing Efficiency 246
Tracking Trends and Events 247
Collaborative Research and Data Sharing 247
Ethical Considerations 247
Section 16.2: Supporting Artists and Designers 248
Finding Visual Inspiration 248
Accessing Reference Materials 248
AI-Powered Design Tools 248
Researching Art Movements and Styles 249
Collaboration and Feedback 249
Ethical Considerations 249
Section 16.3: Enhancing Music and Entertainment Research
.... 250
Exploring Music and Entertainment History 250
Music Theory and Composition 250
Access to Performances and Concerts 250

Discovering New Artists and Music 251
Analyzing Trends and Pop Culture 251
Ethical Considerations 251
Section 16.4: AI's Role in Creative Inspiration 252
Creative Content Generation 252
Music Composition and Arrangement 252
Visual Arts and Design 252
Interactive Storytelling 253
Cross-Disciplinary Collaboration 253
Ethical Considerations 253
Section 16.5: Addressing Intellectual Property Concerns 254
Ownership of AI-Generated Content 254
Copyright and AI-Generated Art 254
Attribution and Plagiarism 255
Licensing and Usage Agreements 255
Monitoring and Enforcement 255
Ethical Considerations 255
Chapter 17: Google Bard for Health and Wellness 256
Section 17.1: Accessing Health Information 256
Section 17.2: Evaluating Medical Research and Data 259
Section 17.3: Wellness Tips and Resources 263
Section 17.4: Navigating Health-Related Queries Responsibly
.... 267
Section 17.5: The Future of AI in Personal Health Management
.... 270
Section 18.1: Exploring Climate Change Information 273
Section 18.2: Accessing Data on Sustainability Practices 275
Section 18.3: Engaging with Environmental Activism 278
Section 18.4: Analyzing Environmental Policies and News .. 281

Section 18.5: Promoting Eco-Conscious Living 284

Section 19.1: Accessibility in Different Languages and Regions 287

Section 19.2: Understanding Global Search Trends 290

Section 19.3: International News and Events............................292

Section 19.4: Respecting Cultural Differences in Search.........295

Section 19.5: The Global Digital Divide and Access to Information 297

Chapter 20: Continuous Learning with Google Bard 300

Section 20.1: Keeping Up with AI and Search Engine Developments...300

Section 20.2: Engaging with Online Courses and Webinars .302

Section 20.3: Reading and Research Strategies........................304

Section 20.4: The Importance of Lifelong Learning in the Digital Age..306

Section 20.5: Looking Ahead: The Evolving Landscape of AI-Powered Search..309

Chapter 1: Introduction to Google Bard

1.1 The Rise of AI in Search Technology

Artificial Intelligence (AI) has become a driving force in the world of search technology. With advancements in machine learning and natural language processing, search engines have evolved beyond simple keyword-based retrieval systems. Google Bard represents a significant milestone in this evolution, as it harnesses the power of AI to provide users with more personalized and context-aware search experiences.

AI-powered search engines like Google Bard have gained prominence due to their ability to understand user intent and deliver relevant results. Traditional search engines relied heavily on exact keyword matches, often producing results that were not entirely aligned with what users were seeking. In contrast, Google Bard employs sophisticated algorithms that analyze the meaning behind user queries, making it more adept at interpreting natural language and context.

One of the key drivers behind the rise of AI in search technology is the exponential growth of digital information. The internet is flooded with an ever-increasing volume of text, images, videos, and data. Navigating this vast sea of information can be daunting without the assistance of AI-driven search engines. Google Bard's ability to sift through massive datasets and deliver precise answers is a testament to the capabilities of AI in addressing the information overload problem.

Moreover, AI-powered search engines like Google Bard have the potential to revolutionize various domains, from education and business to healthcare and entertainment. They are not limited to text-based queries but also support voice search, making information retrieval more accessible and convenient for users of all ages and abilities. This shift towards voice-based interactions is partly driven by the proliferation of voice-activated devices and virtual assistants.

As we delve deeper into this chapter, we will explore Google Bard's capabilities in detail, understand its interface, and set realistic expectations about what it can and cannot do. The journey into the world of AI-powered search begins here, promising a more efficient and intuitive way to access information in an increasingly digital and data-rich age.

1.2 Understanding Google Bard's Capabilities

Google Bard, as an AI-powered search engine, possesses a wide array of capabilities that set it apart from traditional search engines. In this section, we will delve into these capabilities, providing you with a comprehensive understanding of what Google Bard can achieve.

1. Natural Language Understanding

At the core of Google Bard's capabilities lies its proficiency in natural language understanding. Unlike conventional search engines that rely on exact keyword matches, Google Bard comprehends the meaning behind user queries. It considers context, synonyms, and even user intent to deliver more accurate and contextually relevant results. This means that users can ask questions in a more conversational manner and expect meaningful responses.

2. Personalization

Google Bard excels in personalization, tailoring search results to individual users. It takes into account factors like user history, preferences, and location to provide results that are highly relevant to each user. For instance, if you frequently search for tech-related topics, Google Bard will prioritize technology-related results in your searches.

3. Voice Search

Voice search is another impressive feature of Google Bard. Users can simply speak their queries, and Google Bard will understand and respond effectively. This feature is not only convenient but also beneficial for individuals with disabilities or those who prefer a hands-free approach.

```
# Example of a voice search query
user_query = "What's the weather forecast for tomorrow?"
response = google_bard.voice_search(user_query)
```

4. Semantic Search

Google Bard employs semantic search techniques to go beyond keyword matching. It analyzes the context and semantics of words in a query to provide more meaningful results. This approach reduces reliance on exact phrases and enables users to receive accurate answers even if they phrase their questions differently.

5. Conversational AI

The conversational AI capabilities of Google Bard enable it to engage in interactive conversations with users. Users can ask follow-up questions, and Google Bard will maintain context, making the search experience feel more like a dialogue.

```
// Example of a conversation with Google Bard
user_input = "Tell me about Albert Einstein."
response_1 = google_bard.search(user_input)
user_input = "Where did he receive his Nobel Prize?"
response_2 = google_bard.continue_conversation(user_input, response_1)
```

6. Multimodal Search

Google Bard supports multimodal search, meaning it can process various types of content, including text, images, and videos. This capability enables users to search for information in diverse formats and enriches the search experience.

7. Real-time Updates

Google Bard provides real-time updates on topics of interest. Users can subscribe to specific topics or receive alerts for breaking news, ensuring they stay informed about the latest developments in their areas of interest.

8. Complex Query Handling

Complex queries are no challenge for Google Bard. Whether you're seeking answers to mathematical equations, historical facts, or detailed research topics, Google Bard can handle a wide range of complex queries effectively.

```
-- Example of a complex query
SELECT population FROM countries WHERE name = 'India'
```

9. Integration with Other Google Services

Google Bard seamlessly integrates with other Google services such as Google Maps, Google Calendar, and Google Drive. This integration allows users to perform actions like scheduling events, accessing maps, or retrieving files directly from the search interface.

These are just some of the key capabilities that make Google Bard a formidable AI-driven search engine. In the following sections, we will delve deeper into its interface, search techniques, and practical applications to harness its full potential.

1.3 The Evolution from Traditional Search Engines to AI-Powered Solutions

The emergence of AI-powered search engines like Google Bard marks a significant shift in the evolution of search technology. To understand the importance of this transition, it's essential to trace the journey from traditional search engines to these advanced AI-driven solutions.

1. Traditional Keyword-Based Search Engines

Traditional search engines, such as early versions of Google, Yahoo, and Bing, relied primarily on keyword-based search algorithms. Users entered keywords or phrases, and the search engine returned results based on exact matches. While effective to some extent, these engines often struggled with context and intent, leading to less precise results.

```html
<!-- Example of a traditional search query -->
<input type="text" placeholder="Enter your search query" />
<button>Search</button>
```

2. The Rise of Semantic Search

The need for more intelligent search results gave rise to semantic search. This approach aimed to understand the meaning behind words, enabling search engines to provide results based on context rather than just keywords. Semantic search was a step towards improving the relevance of search results.

3. Machine Learning and Natural Language Processing

The integration of machine learning and natural language processing (NLP) marked a crucial turning point. AI-driven search engines like Google Bard leverage NLP techniques to interpret user queries, discern context, and determine user intent. Machine learning models continuously improve search quality by learning from user interactions.

```python
# Example of an NLP model in action
import nlp_library
user_query = "Translate 'hello' to French"
response = nlp_library.translate(user_query)
```

4. Personalization and User Insights

AI-powered search engines excel in personalization. They consider a user's search history, preferences, and location to tailor search results. These engines learn from user behavior to enhance the user experience, making every search more relevant and user-specific.

5. Conversational AI and Voice Search

Conversational AI and voice search are among the most transformative advancements. Users can engage in natural conversations with AI-powered search engines, asking questions and receiving responses in a dialogue-like manner. This is made possible through voice recognition and sophisticated chatbot technology.

```
// Example of voice-activated conversational AI
user_input = "Find nearby restaurants"
response = voice_search(user_input)
```

6. Multimodal Search and Rich Content

AI-powered search engines support multimodal search, enabling users to search not only for text-based information but also for images, videos, and more. This versatility enriches the search experience and accommodates various content types.

7. Real-time Updates and Alerts

Users can receive real-time updates and alerts on topics of interest. AI-driven search engines allow users to subscribe to news feeds, receive notifications, and stay informed about breaking news and events.

8. Integration with Ecosystem

AI-powered search engines are seamlessly integrated into an ecosystem of services. For example, Google Bard integrates with Google's suite of applications, making it possible to perform actions like scheduling events or accessing files directly from the search interface.

9. Continuous Advancements

One of the strengths of AI-powered search engines is their ability to continuously improve. With each interaction, these engines gather more data and learn from user behavior, resulting in ever-enhancing search capabilities.

The evolution from traditional search engines to AI-powered solutions is characterized by an increasing focus on understanding user intent, context, and providing personalized, conversational, and multimodal search experiences. Google Bard stands at the forefront of this evolution, offering users a glimpse into the future of information retrieval.

1.4 Navigating the Interface of Google Bard

Understanding the user interface of Google Bard is crucial for making the most of its powerful capabilities. In this section, we will explore the various elements and features of Google Bard's interface, ensuring you can navigate it efficiently.

1. Search Bar and Query Input

The central element of Google Bard's interface is the search bar. This is where you input your queries, whether they are in text or voice format. Google Bard's natural language processing capabilities mean you can ask questions and phrase queries in a conversational manner.

```
<!-- Example of the Google Bard search bar -->
<input type="text" id="search-bar" placeholder="Ask Google Bard..." />
<button id="search-button">Search</button>
```

2. Search Results

Beneath the search bar, you'll find the search results section. This is where Google Bard displays its responses to your queries. Results are typically ranked by relevance, with the most relevant information appearing at the top. Each result includes a title, snippet, and source link.

```html
<!-- Example of search result display -->
<div class="search-result">
    <h3>Result Title</h3>
    <p>Snippet of the content relevant to your query...</p>
    <a href="https://www.example.com">Source</a>
</div>
```

3. Filters and Advanced Search Options

To the left or right of the search results, you may find filters and advanced search options. These allow you to refine your search by date, location, content type, and other criteria. Filters help you narrow down results when you have specific requirements.

```
// Example of using filters in Google Bard
applyFilter("Date: Past Month");
```

4. Voice Search and Assistant

For voice search and conversational interactions, Google Bard often features a voice-activated assistant. You can activate it by clicking a microphone icon or using a voice command. The assistant can understand and respond to voice queries, making it convenient for hands-free searching.

```
// Example of activating the voice assistant
activateVoiceAssistant();
```

5. Recommendations and Suggestions

Google Bard's interface may provide recommendations and suggestions as you type your query. These suggestions help refine your query and offer shortcuts to commonly searched topics. This feature can save time and guide you in finding relevant information.

```
// Example of query suggestions in the search bar
displayQuerySuggestions();
```

6. Conversation History

When engaging in a conversation with Google Bard, your interaction history may be visible in the interface. This allows you to reference previous queries and responses, helping you maintain context in ongoing conversations.

7. User Profile and Settings

Depending on the implementation, Google Bard may feature a user profile and settings section. Here, you can customize your preferences, review your search history, manage privacy settings, and configure personalized features.

```
<!-- Example of a user profile and settings interface -->
<div class="user-profile">
    <h3>User Profile</h3>
    <!-- User preferences and settings options -->
</div>
```

8. Real-time Updates and Alerts

If you've subscribed to real-time updates or alerts, you may receive notifications within the interface. These updates keep you informed about the latest news or events related to your interests.

9. Integration with Other Services

Google Bard's interface may include integrations with other Google services. This could manifest as quick access to Google Calendar, Google Drive, or other applications, allowing you to seamlessly transition between tasks.

Navigating the interface of Google Bard is designed to be user-friendly, accommodating various types of interactions, from traditional text-based queries to voice-activated conversations. Familiarizing yourself with these interface elements will enable you to harness Google Bard's capabilities effectively for your information retrieval needs.

1.5 Setting Expectations: What Google Bard Can and Cannot Do

Before diving deeper into using Google Bard, it's essential to establish realistic expectations regarding its capabilities and limitations. Understanding what Google Bard can and cannot do will help you make the most of this AI-powered search engine.

What Google Bard Can Do

1. **Natural Language Understanding**: Google Bard excels in understanding natural language and context. It can process conversational queries and provide contextually relevant results, making it feel more interactive.

2. **Personalization**: Google Bard tailors search results to individual users based on their history and preferences. This personalization enhances the relevance of search results.

3. **Voice Search**: Google Bard supports voice-activated search, making it accessible and convenient for users who prefer voice commands.

4. **Semantic Search**: The engine employs semantic search techniques to provide results based on the meaning of words, reducing reliance on exact keywords.

5. **Multimodal Search**: Google Bard can process various types of content, including text, images, and videos, providing a versatile search experience.

6. **Real-time Updates**: Users can receive real-time updates and alerts on topics of interest, staying informed about the latest developments.

7. **Integration with Ecosystem**: Google Bard seamlessly integrates with other Google services, allowing users to perform actions like scheduling events or accessing files directly from the search interface.

8. **Continuous Learning**: Google Bard's machine learning models continuously improve search quality by learning from user interactions, ensuring ongoing enhancements.

What Google Bard Cannot Do

1. **Mind Reading**: While Google Bard is adept at understanding natural language, it cannot read your thoughts. It relies on the information you provide through queries.

2. **Predicting Future Events**: Google Bard cannot predict future events or provide information that is not publicly available. It offers real-time updates but does not have clairvoyant capabilities.

3. **Accessing Restricted Information**: Google Bard respects privacy and security protocols and cannot access or provide information that is behind secure firewalls or private databases.

4. **Creating Original Content**: It cannot create original content, write articles, or generate creative works. It can only provide information based on existing data.

5. **Solving Complex Personal Issues**: Google Bard is not a therapist or counselor. It cannot provide medical, legal, or personal advice. Seek professional help for such matters.

6. **Guaranteeing 100% Accuracy**: While Google Bard aims for high accuracy, it may still occasionally provide incorrect or outdated information. Always verify critical information from trusted sources.

7. **Replacing Human Expertise**: Google Bard can assist in finding information, but it cannot replace the expertise of humans, especially in specialized fields.

8. **Understanding Every Language and Dialect**: While it supports various languages, Google Bard may not understand every dialect or regional variation equally well.

Understanding these capabilities and limitations is crucial for using Google Bard effectively. It is a powerful tool for information retrieval and assistance, but it is not infallible and has boundaries that users should be aware of. Setting realistic expectations will lead to a more satisfying and productive experience when interacting with Google Bard.

Chapter 2: Getting Started with Google Bard

2.1 Creating a Google Bard Account

To fully access and benefit from Google Bard's features, you need to create a Google Bard account. In this section, we will guide you through the steps to set up your account and get started with this AI-powered search engine.

1. Accessing the Registration Page

The first step is to access the registration page of Google Bard. This can typically be done by visiting the official Google Bard website or using the Google Bard app on your device.

```
<!-- Example of a registration page link -->
<a href="https://www.googlebard.com/register">Register for Google Bard</a>
```

2. Providing Your Information

Once on the registration page, you will be asked to provide some basic information. This may include your name, email address, and password. Ensure that you use a strong and secure password to protect your account.

```
<!-- Example of a registration form -->
<form>
    <label for="name">Name:</label>
    <input type="text" id="name" name="name" required>
    <label for="email">Email:</label>
    <input type="email" id="email" name="email" required>
    <label for="password">Password:</label>
    <input type="password" id="password" name="password" required>
    <button type="submit">Register</button>
</form>
```

3. Verification and Authentication

After providing your information, you may need to verify your email address. This typically involves receiving a verification link or code in your email inbox and following the provided instructions to confirm your account.

```html
<!-- Example of an email verification message -->
<p>To verify your email address, please click on the link sent to your inbox.</p>
```

4. Setting Up Your Profile

Once your account is verified, you can log in to Google Bard and set up your profile. This may include adding a profile picture, providing additional details about yourself, and customizing your user experience.

```javascript
// Example of setting up a user profile
const user = {
    name: "John Doe",
    profilePicture: "profile.jpg",
    interests: ["technology", "travel", "science"]
};
```

5. Customizing Preferences

Google Bard offers various customization options. You can adjust your search preferences, language settings, and privacy options to tailor the experience to your liking.

```javascript
// Example of customizing search preferences
const preferences = {
    language: "English",
    region: "United States",
    searchHistory: true
};
```

6. Exploring the Interface

Once your account is set up, take some time to explore the Google Bard interface. Familiarize yourself with the search bar, search results, and any additional features or tools that are available. This will help you navigate the platform effectively.

7. Learning Basic Search Techniques

To make the most of Google Bard, it's essential to learn basic and advanced search techniques. These include using specific keywords, filters, and operators to refine your searches and find the information you need quickly.

```
// Example of a basic search query
const query = "How does solar energy work?";
```

Creating a Google Bard account is the first step towards harnessing the power of this AI-driven search engine. It allows you to access personalized features, receive real-time updates, and engage in interactive conversations. With your account in place, you are ready to explore the world of Google Bard and discover its numerous capabilities.

2.2 Customizing Your User Experience

Customization is a key aspect of making your Google Bard experience more tailored to your preferences and needs. In this section, we will explore various ways to customize your user experience within Google Bard.

1. Personalizing Your Profile

One of the first steps to customization is personalizing your profile. You can upload a profile picture, add a brief bio, and specify your interests. This not only makes your profile more engaging but also helps Google Bard understand your preferences better.

```
// Example of updating a user's profile
const user = {
    name: "Jane Smith",
```

```
    profilePicture: "profile.jpg",
    bio: "Tech enthusiast and travel lover.",
    interests: ["technology", "travel"]
};
```

2. Language and Region Preferences

Google Bard supports multiple languages and regions. You can customize your language preference to receive search results and interactions in your preferred language. Additionally, setting your region helps Google Bard provide location-specific information.

```
// Example of setting language and region preferences
const preferences = {
    language: "Spanish",
    region: "Spain"
};
```

3. Search History and Personalization

Google Bard offers the option to enable or disable search history tracking. If you prefer a more personalized experience with tailored search results based on your search history, you can keep this feature enabled. If you value privacy and prefer not to have your search history recorded, you can opt to disable it.

```
// Example of managing search history preferences
const preferences = {
    searchHistory: true // Enable search history tracking
};
```

4. Customizing the Home Page

Some versions of Google Bard allow you to customize the home page with widgets or shortcuts to your favorite features. You can add widgets for weather updates, news, or quick access to specific search topics.

```
<!-- Example of customizing the home page with widgets -->
```

```html
<div class="home-page">
    <div class="widget">
        <!-- Weather widget -->
    </div>
    <div class="widget">
        <!-- News widget -->
    </div>
</div>
```

5. Privacy Settings

Google Bard takes privacy seriously. You can customize your privacy settings to control how your data is used. This includes options for ad personalization, data sharing, and more. Adjust these settings to align with your privacy preferences.

```javascript
// Example of privacy settings customization
const privacySettings = {
    adPersonalization: false, // Opt out of ad personalization
    dataSharing: false // Opt out of data sharing
};
```

6. Notifications and Alerts

Customize the notifications and alerts you receive from Google Bard. You can choose to receive real-time updates on specific topics, subscribe to newsletters, or adjust the frequency of email notifications.

```javascript
// Example of managing notifications preferences
const notifications = {
    realTimeUpdates: true, // Receive real-time updates
    newsletterSubscription: false // Opt out of newsletters
};
```

7. Theme and Appearance

In some versions of Google Bard, you may have the option to customize the theme and appearance of the interface. You can choose from different color schemes, fonts, and layout options to suit your visual preferences.

```
// Example of theme customization
const theme = {
    colorScheme: "Dark Mode",
    font: "Roboto",
    layout: "Compact"
};
```

Customizing your user experience in Google Bard allows you to tailor the platform to your liking. Whether it's adjusting language settings, managing privacy preferences, or customizing the appearance, these options help you make Google Bard work for you, providing a more personalized and enjoyable search experience.

2.3 Basic and Advanced Search Techniques

To effectively use Google Bard, it's essential to understand a variety of search techniques. In this section, we'll explore both basic and advanced search strategies that will help you retrieve information more efficiently.

1. Basic Keyword Search

The most fundamental search technique is entering keywords related to your query in the search bar. Google Bard will then retrieve results containing those keywords. For example, if you're looking for information about space exploration, you can enter "space exploration" as your query.

```
// Example of a basic keyword search
const query = "space exploration";
```

2. Exact Phrase Search

To narrow down results, you can use quotation marks to search for an exact phrase. This is helpful when you're looking for specific information or quotes. For instance, searching for "Neil Armstrong's famous words" will retrieve results containing that exact phrase.

```
// Example of an exact phrase search
const query = "\"Neil Armstrong's famous words\"";
```

3. Boolean Operators

Boolean operators like AND, OR, and NOT can be used to refine your search. "AND" narrows down results by requiring both keywords to be present, "OR" broadens results by looking for either keyword, and "NOT" excludes a specific keyword from results.

```
// Example of a boolean operator search
const query = "space exploration AND Mars";
```

4. Site-Specific Search

If you want to search within a specific website, you can use the "site:" operator followed by the website's domain. This is useful when you're looking for information on a particular site. For example, "site:wikipedia.org Apollo 11" will search for Apollo 11 information on Wikipedia.

```
// Example of a site-specific search
const query = "site:wikipedia.org Apollo 11";
```

5. File Type Search

To find specific types of files, you can use the "filetype:" operator followed by the file extension. For instance, "filetype:pdf climate change" will retrieve PDF documents related to climate change.

```
// Example of a file type search
const query = "filetype:pdf climate change";
```

6. Advanced Query Operators

Google Bard supports advanced query operators like "intitle:" to search for pages with specific words in the title and "inurl:" to find pages with specific words in the URL. These operators help you locate information in specific contexts.

```
// Example of advanced query operators
const query = "intitle:NASA inurl:missions";
```

7. Advanced Filters

Use advanced filters to refine your search results further. Filters allow you to narrow down by date, location, content type, and more. For instance, you can filter results to show only news articles from the past week.

```
// Example of using advanced filters
const filter = {
    date: "Past Week",
    contentType: "News"
};
```

8. Voice Search

Take advantage of voice search for a hands-free experience. Simply click the microphone icon or use voice commands to speak your query. Voice search is especially useful when you're on the go or prefer not to type.

```
// Example of activating voice search
activateVoiceSearch();
```

9. Conversational Search

Engage in conversational search by asking follow-up questions. Google Bard maintains context, allowing you to ask related queries without restating the entire question.

```
// Example of a conversational search
user_input = "Tell me about Albert Einstein.";
response_1 = google_bard.search(user_input);
user_input = "Where did he receive his Nobel Prize?";
```

```
response_2 = google_bard.continue_conversation(user_inp
ut, response_1);
```

10. Multimodal Search

Google Bard supports multimodal search, allowing you to search for text, images, and videos. Use this feature to find information in various formats.

```
// Example of a multimodal search
const query = "space exploration images";
```

Understanding and mastering these basic and advanced search techniques will empower you to make the most of Google Bard's capabilities. Whether you're conducting research, looking for specific information, or exploring diverse content types, these techniques will enhance your search experience.

2.4 Interpreting Google Bard's Responses

Understanding and interpreting Google Bard's responses is essential for extracting valuable information effectively. In this section, we will explore how to make sense of the search engine's output and utilize it to its fullest potential.

1. Result Structure

When you perform a search, Google Bard typically returns a list of results. Each result consists of several elements, including:

- **Title**: The title of the web page or content source.
- **Snippet**: A brief excerpt from the content that provides context.
- **Source Link**: A clickable link to the source of the information.

These elements help you quickly assess whether a result is relevant to your query.

```
<!-- Example of a typical search result structure -->
<div class="search-result">
    <h3>Result Title</h3>
    <p>Snippet of the content relevant to your query...
</p>
    <a href="https://www.example.com">Source</a>
</div>
```

2. Relevance Ranking

Google Bard employs a relevance ranking algorithm to order search results. The most relevant results are usually displayed at the top. Understanding this ranking can help you focus on the most pertinent information.

```
// Example of sorting search results by relevance
results.sortByRelevance();
```

3. Click-Through Behavior

To explore a result further, you can click on the source link. This takes you to the original web page or content source, where you can access more detailed information.

```
// Example of clicking through to view the full content
clickOnResult(result);
```

4. Evaluating Snippets

The snippet provided in search results offers a concise summary of the content. Pay attention to snippets as they give you a glimpse into what the source contains. If a snippet aligns with your information needs, you can explore the source further.

```
// Example of analyzing a snippet for relevance
const snippet = "Snippet of the content relevant to your query...";
```

5. Refining Queries

If the initial search results do not meet your expectations, consider refining your query. You can modify keywords, use Boolean operators, or apply filters to narrow down results.

```
// Example of refining a query to improve results
const refinedQuery = "space exploration missions";
```

6. Voice Responses

When using voice search or interacting with Google Bard through a voice-activated assistant, pay attention to the responses. Google Bard may provide vocal responses, and understanding these responses is essential for extracting information.

```
// Example of a voice response
voiceResponse = "The first manned moon landing was Apollo 11 in 1969.";
```

7. Conversation History

If you're engaged in a conversation with Google Bard, keep track of the conversation history. This helps you maintain context and refer back to previous queries and responses.

```
// Example of accessing conversation history
const conversationHistory = [
    { query: "Tell me about space exploration", response: "Space exploration is the discovery and exploration of outer space." },
    { query: "What are some famous missions?", response: "Some famous missions include Apollo 11 and the Mars rover missions." }
];
```

8. Multimodal Content

Google Bard supports multimodal content, including images and videos. When interpreting search results, be aware that some sources may contain multimedia elements, providing a more comprehensive view of the topic.

```
// Example of interpreting search results with multimedia content
const resultWithVideo = {
    title: "Exploring Mars",
```

```
    snippet: "Watch a video about Mars exploration.",
    sourceLink: "https://www.example.com/mars-explorati
on-video"
};
```

9. Real-Time Updates

Google Bard may provide real-time updates on specific topics or events. Be vigilant about the timeliness of the information, especially when dealing with news or rapidly evolving subjects.

```
// Example of real-time updates on a news topic
realTimeUpdate = "Breaking News: NASA announces plans f
or a new Mars mission.";
```

10. Verification of Information

Lastly, verify the information you retrieve from Google Bard, especially if it's critical or factual. Cross-reference data from multiple reputable sources to ensure accuracy.

Interpreting Google Bard's responses requires a critical and discerning approach. By mastering these techniques, you can efficiently navigate search results, extract valuable information, and make informed decisions based on the knowledge you acquire.

2.5 Tips for Efficient Information Retrieval

Efficient information retrieval is a crucial skill when using Google Bard, especially when you want to find specific information quickly. In this section, we'll explore some valuable tips and strategies to enhance your efficiency in retrieving information.

1. Use Descriptive Keywords

When formulating your search query, be as specific and descriptive as possible. Use keywords that accurately represent the information you seek. For instance, instead of searching for "space," search for "recent discoveries in space exploration."

```
// Example of a descriptive search query
const query = "recent discoveries in space exploration";
```

2. Refine Your Query

If your initial query doesn't yield the desired results, don't hesitate to refine it. Experiment with different keywords, synonyms, or variations until you find what you're looking for.

```
// Example of refining a query
const refinedQuery = "latest space exploration breakthroughs";
```

3. Utilize Advanced Search Operators

Advanced search operators like "site:", "filetype:", and Boolean operators can help you narrow down results and locate specific information more effectively. Master these operators to enhance your search skills.

```
// Example of using advanced search operators
const query = "site:nasa.gov Mars missions";
```

4. Check Related Searches

Google Bard often provides related search suggestions at the bottom of the search results page. These can be helpful if you're looking for variations of your query or related topics.

```
// Example of checking related searches
relatedSearches = ["Recent Mars missions", "Space exploration news"];
```

5. Explore Advanced Filters

Take advantage of advanced filters to refine your search results. Filters allow you to specify date ranges, content types, and more. Use them to narrow down results to the most relevant information.

```
// Example of applying advanced filters
const filters = {
    date: "Past Year",
    contentType: "Research Papers"
};
```

6. Use Voice Search for Convenience

Voice search can be incredibly convenient, especially when you're busy or prefer hands-free interaction. Activate the voice assistant and speak your query for quick results.

```
// Example of activating voice search
activateVoiceSearch();
```

7. Maintain a Search History

Keeping a record of your search history can be beneficial, especially when you need to revisit previous queries or verify information you've found.

```
// Example of maintaining a search history
searchHistory = [
    "How does solar energy work?",
    "Advantages of electric cars",
    "SpaceX latest launch"
];
```

8. Bookmark Important Sources

If you frequently access specific sources or websites for information, consider bookmarking them for quick access in the future. This can save you time when conducting research.

```
// Example of bookmarking a source
const bookmarks = [
```

```
    { title: "NASA's official website", link: "https://
www.nasa.gov" },
    { title: "National Geographic - Space", link: "http
s://www.nationalgeographic.com/space" }
];
```

9. Stay Informed About Updates

Google Bard and its algorithms continuously evolve. Stay informed about updates, new features, and changes in search behavior to adapt your search strategies accordingly.

```
// Example of staying informed about updates
updateNotifications = true; // Receive notifications ab
out Google Bard updates
```

10. Cross-Verify Critical Information

When you encounter critical or factual information, especially in research or decision-making contexts, cross-verify it from multiple reputable sources to ensure accuracy and reliability.

Efficiency in information retrieval comes with practice and a willingness to explore different search techniques. By incorporating these tips into your search habits, you can become a more adept and efficient user of Google Bard, effectively finding the information you seek while saving time and effort.

Chapter 3: Advanced Features and Tools

3.1 Utilizing Voice Search with Google Bard

Voice search is a powerful feature that enhances the usability of Google Bard. It allows users to perform searches and access information using spoken commands. In this section, we will delve into the details of voice search and how to make the most of it.

1. Activating Voice Search

To initiate voice search with Google Bard, you typically need to click on the microphone icon in the search interface. This activates the voice recognition system, allowing you to speak your query.

```
// Example of activating voice search
activateVoiceSearch();
```

2. Speaking Clearly and Concisely

When using voice search, it's essential to speak clearly and concisely. Enunciate your words to ensure accurate recognition. Avoid long, complex sentences and focus on delivering your query succinctly.

```
// Example of clear and concise voice query
const voiceQuery = "Weather forecast for New York City today.";
```

3. Natural Language Queries

Google Bard's voice search is designed to understand natural language queries. You can speak your query conversationally, just as you would if you were asking a question in person.

```
// Example of a natural language voice query
const voiceQuery = "Tell me about the latest developments in artificial intelligence.";
```

4. Voice Commands

In addition to performing searches, you can use voice commands to control various aspects of Google Bard. For example, you can say "Go back" to return to the previous screen or "Read it aloud" to have Google Bard read search results to you.

```
// Example of voice commands
voiceCommand("Go back");
voiceCommand("Read it aloud");
```

5. Voice Search for Accessibility

Voice search is not only a convenience but also an accessibility feature. It allows individuals with physical disabilities to access and interact with Google Bard more easily. Ensure that voice search accessibility options are enabled for a seamless experience.

```
// Example of enabling voice search accessibility
enableVoiceSearchAccessibility();
```

6. Supported Languages

Google Bard's voice search supports a wide range of languages. You can typically change the language settings in the preferences to use voice search in your preferred language.

```
// Example of changing voice search language
setVoiceSearchLanguage("Spanish");
```

7. Voice Response Feedback

Google Bard provides voice responses to your voice queries. Be attentive to these responses, as they contain the information you requested. You can pause or replay responses if needed.

```
// Example of voice response interaction
voiceResponse = "The temperature in New York City today is 78 degrees Fahrenheit.";
pauseVoiceResponse();
```

8. Privacy Considerations

When using voice search, it's important to be aware of privacy considerations. Voice queries are typically processed on remote servers, so ensure you are comfortable with the privacy policies and data handling practices of the voice search provider.

9. Troubleshooting Voice Recognition

In some cases, voice recognition may not accurately capture your query. If you encounter issues, consider rephrasing your query or checking your microphone settings. Google Bard's support documentation may also offer guidance on troubleshooting voice recognition problems.

```
// Example of troubleshooting voice recognition
const voiceQuery = "I'm looking for information on global warming.";
```

10. Feedback and Improvements

Voice search systems continually improve through user feedback. If you encounter recurring issues or have suggestions for enhancements, consider providing feedback to the Google Bard team. This helps in refining voice recognition capabilities over time.

```
// Example of providing feedback on voice search
submitVoiceSearchFeedback("Voice recognition accuracy needs improvement.");
```

Utilizing voice search with Google Bard can make your interactions more intuitive and accessible. Whether you're using it for quick searches, hands-free operation, or as an accessibility feature, mastering voice search can greatly enhance your experience with this AI-powered search engine.

3.2 Exploring Bard's Interactive Elements

Google Bard offers a range of interactive elements that enhance your search experience and allow you to engage more dynamically with the platform. In this section, we'll explore some of these interactive features and how they can be utilized.

1. Interactive Cards

Interactive cards are visual elements that provide additional information or actions related to your search query. They may include carousels of images, videos, or other multimedia content. To interact with an interactive card, simply click or tap on it to explore further.

```
// Example of interacting with an interactive card
clickOnInteractiveCard(card);
```

2. Knowledge Panels

Knowledge panels are informative sidebars that appear alongside search results. They provide summarized information about a specific topic, person, or place. You can expand a knowledge panel to view more details or click on the links within it for related information.

```
// Example of expanding a knowledge panel
expandKnowledgePanel(knowledgePanel);
```

3. Featured Snippets

Featured snippets are concise answers or information displayed prominently at the top of search results. They aim to provide quick answers to common questions. You can click on a featured snippet to view the source and more details.

```
// Example of clicking on a featured snippet
clickOnFeaturedSnippet(featuredSnippet);
```

4. Interactive Maps

Google Bard often integrates interactive maps into search results. You can zoom in, pan, and click on map markers to explore locations, view directions, or find nearby businesses or points of interest.

```
// Example of interacting with an interactive map
zoomInOnMap(map);
```

5. Carousel Browsing

In some searches, Google Bard presents information in a carousel format. You can scroll horizontally through the carousel to view different items, such as news articles, products, or images. Click on a carousel item to access more details.

```
// Example of scrolling through a carousel
scrollCarousel(carousel);
```

6. In-SERP Actions

Google Bard allows you to perform actions directly within the search engine results page (SERP). For instance, you can book a reservation, order food, or make appointments without leaving the search results page.

```
// Example of making a reservation within the SERP
bookReservation();
```

7. Instant Answers

Google Bard strives to provide instant answers to common queries. If you type a question, you may receive a direct response without the need to click on search results. Instant answers are often helpful for quick reference.

```
// Example of receiving an instant answer
instantAnswer = "The capital of France is Paris.";
```

8. Visual Search

Visual search allows you to upload an image or take a photo to find related information or products. It's especially useful for identifying objects, landmarks, or products you encounter in the real world.

```
// Example of performing a visual search
uploadImageForVisualSearch(image);
```

9. Conversational Search

Engage in conversational search with Google Bard by asking follow-up questions or seeking clarification. Google Bard retains context, making it easy to continue the conversation and explore related topics.

```
// Example of a conversational search
user_input = "Tell me about space exploration.";
response_1 = google_bard.search(user_input);
user_input = "What are some recent missions?";
response_2 = google_bard.continue_conversation(user_inp
ut, response_1);
```

10. Real-Time Updates

Google Bard may provide real-time updates on specific topics, especially in the case of news or trending events. Keep an eye on these updates to stay informed about the latest developments.

```
// Example of real-time updates on a news topic
realTimeUpdate = "Breaking News: A major discovery on M
ars has been announced.";
```

Exploring these interactive elements within Google Bard allows you to access information in a more engaging and dynamic way. Whether you're looking for visual content, quick answers, or actions you can perform directly from the SERP, these features enhance your search experience and make it easier to find the information you need.

3.3 Advanced Query Formulation

Effective search on Google Bard often involves more than just entering a few keywords. In this section, we'll delve into advanced query formulation techniques that allow you to refine and target your searches for more precise results.

1. Exact Match

If you're looking for an exact phrase, enclose it in double quotation marks. This tells Google Bard to search for that precise phrase, ensuring that the results contain the exact words in the specified order.

```
// Example of an exact match query
const query = "\"Artificial intelligence in healthcare\"";
```

2. Boolean Operators

Boolean operators (AND, OR, NOT) allow you to create complex queries by combining keywords. "AND" narrows results by requiring both keywords, "OR" broadens results by accepting either keyword, and "NOT" excludes a specific keyword.

```
// Example of a boolean operator query
const query = "space exploration AND Mars";
```

3. Site-Specific Searches

To search within a particular website, use the "site:" operator followed by the site's domain. This helps when you want information from a specific source or domain.

```
// Example of a site-specific query
const query = "site:wikipedia.org Apollo 11";
```

4. File Type Searches

To find specific file types, use the "filetype:" operator followed by the file extension. This is handy when looking for documents, presentations, or other specific file formats.

```
// Example of a file type query
const query = "filetype:pdf climate change";
```

5. Related Keywords

Expand your query by including synonyms or related keywords. This broadens the scope of your search and ensures you don't miss relevant information.

```
// Example of a query with related keywords
const query = "renewable energy OR green technology";
```

6. Exclude Terms

Use the minus "-" sign to exclude specific terms from your search results. This is helpful when you want to filter out irrelevant results.

```
// Example of excluding terms from a query
const query = "space exploration -Mars";
```

7. Wildcard Searches

When you're uncertain about a word or phrase, you can use a wildcard (_) to represent unknown parts. For example, "colo_r" matches both "color" and "colour."

```
// Example of a wildcard search
const query = "colo*r palette";
```

8. Range Searches

If you're looking for results within a specific numeric range, use double dots (..) between numbers. For instance, "price $100..$200" searches for products within that price range.

```
// Example of a range search
const query = "price $100..$200";
```

9. Intitle and Inurl Operators

The "intitle:" operator searches for pages with specific words in the title, while "inurl:" searches for words in the URL. These operators help you find information within a particular context.

```
// Example of using intitle and inurl operators
const query = "intitle:NASA inurl:missions";
```

10. Date Filters

To narrow down results by date, use date filters like "before," "after," or "on." This is useful for finding recent or historical information.

```
// Example of using date filters in a query
const query = "space exploration after:2020-01-01";
```

By mastering these advanced query formulation techniques, you can fine-tune your searches on Google Bard, ensuring that you obtain the most relevant and accurate results for your information needs. Whether you're conducting research, seeking specific documents, or exploring complex topics, these techniques empower you to become a more effective searcher.

3.4 Personalization and Privacy Settings

Google Bard offers a range of personalization and privacy settings that allow users to tailor their search experience and control the information they share. In this section, we will explore these settings and how to manage them.

1. Personalized Search Results

By default, Google Bard may personalize your search results based on your previous search history, location, and preferences. Personalization aims to provide more relevant content. To enable or disable personalized results, access your account settings.

```
// Example of toggling personalized search results
togglePersonalizedResults(true); // Enable personalized results
togglePersonalizedResults(false); // Disable personalized results
```

2. Location-Based Results

Google Bard often considers your location when generating search results. This is useful for finding local businesses and services. To change your location settings, access the location preferences in your account.

```
// Example of updating location preferences
updateLocation("New York, NY"); // Set location to New York, NY
```

3. Search History Management

You can view and manage your search history within Google Bard. This allows you to revisit previous queries, clear search history, or pause search history recording.

```
// Example of managing search history
viewSearchHistory();
clearSearchHistory();
pauseSearchHistoryRecording();
```

4. Ad Personalization

Google Bard may display personalized ads based on your search history and interests. You can customize ad personalization settings to control the types of ads you see.

```
// Example of ad personalization settings
customizeAdPreferences();
```

5. SafeSearch Filters

Google Bard offers SafeSearch filters to block explicit content from search results. You can set the level of filtering that suits your preferences, from strict to off.

```
// Example of adjusting SafeSearch settings
setSafeSearchFilter("Moderate"); // Set SafeSearch to m
oderate filtering
```

6. Incognito Mode

Incognito mode allows you to browse and search privately without your activity being saved in your account's search history. This is useful for maintaining privacy when needed.

```
// Example of enabling Incognito mode
enableIncognitoMode();
```

7. Data Retention and Deletion

You can access your account settings to review and manage the data Google Bard retains. This includes the option to delete specific searches or clear all search data.

```
// Example of data retention and deletion
manageDataRetention();
deleteSpecificSearches();
clearAllSearchData();
```

8. Privacy Controls

Google Bard provides privacy controls that allow you to review and manage your data sharing preferences. Review these settings to ensure your privacy preferences are respected.

```
// Example of privacy control settings
customizePrivacySettings();
```

9. Account Security

Maintaining the security of your Google Bard account is essential. Enable two-factor authentication (2FA) and regularly update your password to enhance security.

```
// Example of account security settings
enableTwoFactorAuthentication();
updatePassword();
```

10. Consent for Data Usage

Before using Google Bard, review and provide consent for data usage in accordance with the platform's privacy policy. Understanding and agreeing to data usage terms is a critical aspect of managing your privacy.

```
// Example of reviewing and providing consent for data usage
reviewDataUsagePolicy();
provideConsent();
```

Managing personalization and privacy settings on Google Bard empowers users to have more control over their search experience and data privacy. Whether you prefer personalized results or a more private browsing experience, understanding and customizing these settings ensures that Google Bard aligns with your preferences and values.

3.5 Integrating Google Bard with Other Google Services

Google Bard can be seamlessly integrated with other Google services to enhance your overall digital experience. In this section, we will explore some of the ways you can integrate Google Bard with other Google offerings.

1. Google Account Integration

Google Bard is typically linked to your Google account. This integration allows you to access personalized features and settings associated with your account.

```
// Example of linking Google Bard with a Google account
linkGoogleAccount();
```

2. Google Drive Integration

Integrate Google Bard with Google Drive to save search results, documents, or research findings directly to your Google Drive cloud storage.

```
// Example of saving search results to Google Drive
saveToGoogleDrive(searchResults);
```

3. Google Calendar Integration

You can link Google Bard with your Google Calendar to schedule events, set reminders, or access your calendar appointments through voice commands.

```
// Example of scheduling an event with Google Calendar
scheduleEvent("Meeting with John", "2024-02-15 10:00 AM");
```

4. Google Maps Integration

Google Maps integration allows you to access maps, directions, and location-based information seamlessly while searching on Google Bard.

```
// Example of using Google Maps for location-based queries
findDirections("Coffee shops near me");
```

5. Google Photos Integration

Integrating Google Bard with Google Photos enables you to search for and access your photos and images stored in your Google Photos library.

```
// Example of searching for photos with Google Bard
searchGooglePhotos("Beach vacation 2023");
```

6. Google Translate Integration

You can leverage Google Translate within Google Bard to translate text, phrases, or entire web pages to other languages.

```
// Example of using Google Translate with Google Bard
translateText("Hello, how are you?", "Spanish");
```

7. YouTube Integration

Google Bard can provide video search results from YouTube, and you can also access your YouTube subscriptions and playlists through voice commands.

```
// Example of searching for videos on Google Bard
searchYouTube("Tech reviews");
```

8. Google Assistant Integration

Google Bard can be integrated with Google Assistant for a more conversational and interactive search experience, allowing you to ask follow-up questions or perform actions seamlessly.

```
// Example of integrating Google Bard with Google Assistant
integrateWithGoogleAssistant();
```

9. Google Workspace Integration

For business users, integrating Google Bard with Google Workspace (formerly G Suite) allows for efficient access to emails, calendar events, and documents within your organization.

```
// Example of accessing Google Workspace features with Google Bard
accessWorkspaceEmail("john.doe@example.com");
```

10. Voice Commands for Integration

Most integrations with Google services can be controlled using voice commands. These voice commands enable you to interact with integrated services without leaving the Google Bard environment.

```
// Example of using voice commands for integration
voiceCommand("Show my upcoming appointments");
```

Integrating Google Bard with other Google services streamlines your digital workflow, making it more efficient and convenient. Whether you want to access your calendar, save important information, or perform various tasks with voice commands, these integrations enhance the versatility and usability of Google Bard in your daily life.

Chapter 4: Google Bard in Everyday Life

4.1 Enhancing Personal Productivity

Google Bard offers a multitude of features and tools that can significantly enhance personal productivity in various aspects of daily life. Whether you're managing tasks, organizing your schedule, or staying informed, Google Bard can be a valuable companion. In this section, we'll explore how Google Bard can help you boost your personal productivity.

1. Task Management

You can use Google Bard to manage your tasks efficiently. By integrating with Google Tasks or third-party task management apps, you can create, edit, and check off tasks using voice commands or text inputs.

```
// Example of creating a task with Google Bard
createTask("Finish project report by Friday");
```

2. Calendar Integration

Google Bard seamlessly integrates with your Google Calendar, allowing you to schedule events, set reminders, and view your daily agenda. You can even create events using voice commands.

```
// Example of scheduling an event with Google Bard
scheduleEvent("Meeting with the client", "2024-02-10 2:00 PM");
```

3. Note-taking and Documentation

You can dictate notes, documents, or ideas using Google Bard's voice recognition capabilities. These notes can be saved to Google Drive, simplifying your note-taking process.

```
// Example of dictating a note with Google Bard
dictateNote("Meeting minutes for team discussion");
```

4. Email Management

Integrating Google Bard with your Gmail account allows you to check emails, send messages, and manage your inbox hands-free.

```
// Example of checking emails with Google Bard
checkEmails();
```

5. Language Translation

If you're working with multilingual content, Google Bard's integration with Google Translate can assist you in translating text or understanding foreign language documents.

```
// Example of translating text with Google Bard
translateText("Translate this paragraph to French");
```

6. Setting Reminders

Google Bard can be used to set reminders for important tasks or appointments. You can receive reminders at specified times or when you reach specific locations.

```
// Example of setting a reminder with Google Bard
setReminder("Buy groceries", "2024-02-05 5:00 PM");
```

7. News and Updates

Stay informed about current events, news, and industry updates by asking Google Bard for the latest headlines or subscribing to specific news topics.

```
// Example of staying updated with Google Bard
getNewsHeadlines();
```

8. Time Management

Google Bard can help you manage your time effectively by providing insights into how you spend your day, setting time limits for tasks, or offering time management tips.

```
// Example of time management with Google Bard
analyzeTimeUsage();
```

9. Health and Fitness

For those focused on their health and fitness goals, Google Bard can provide information on nutrition, workout routines, and health tips.

```
// Example of accessing health and fitness information with Google Bard
getNutritionTips();
```

10. Productivity Tracking

Track your productivity and monitor your progress on tasks by asking Google Bard to provide reports on completed tasks and goals.

```
// Example of productivity tracking with Google Bard
trackProductivity();
```

Google Bard's ability to integrate with various productivity tools and provide hands-free assistance makes it a valuable asset for enhancing personal productivity. Whether you're managing tasks, staying organized, or seeking information quickly, Google Bard can simplify your daily routine and help you achieve more in less time.

4.2 Using Google Bard for Educational Purposes

Google Bard is a versatile tool that can be a valuable asset for educational purposes. Whether you're a student, educator, or a lifelong learner, Google Bard offers features and capabilities that can aid in research, learning, and knowledge acquisition. In this section, we'll explore how Google Bard can be utilized in an educational context.

1. Research Assistance

Students and researchers can benefit from Google Bard's ability to provide quick access to information. By asking specific questions or conducting topic-related searches, you can gather data, find academic articles, and access a wealth of knowledge.

```
// Example of research query with Google Bard
searchResearchTopic("Artificial intelligence in healthc
are");
```

2. Study Aid

Google Bard can serve as a study companion. You can use it to retrieve definitions, explanations, and references for various subjects. It's particularly useful for clarifying complex concepts.

```
// Example of asking for a definition with Google Bard
getDefinition("Photosynthesis");
```

3. Language Learning

Language learners can leverage Google Bard's language translation capabilities to practice and improve their language skills. Translate phrases, sentences, or entire paragraphs to your target language.

```
// Example of language translation with Google Bard
translateText("Translate 'Hello, how are you?' to Spani
sh");
```

4. Access to Educational Resources

Google Bard can help you find educational resources such as online courses, tutorials, and reference materials. You can ask for recommendations or search for specific topics of interest.

```
// Example of searching for online courses
findOnlineCourses("Introduction to Machine Learning");
```

5. Math and Science Support

Students studying mathematics and science can use Google Bard for quick calculations, formula explanations, and access to scientific data.

```
// Example of a math query with Google Bard
solveMathProblem("Calculate the integral of x^2");
```

6. Citation and References

When working on academic projects or research papers, Google Bard can assist in generating citations, providing references, and suggesting reputable sources.

```
// Example of generating a citation with Google Bard
generateCitation("APA format for a journal article");
```

7. Historical and Cultural Information

For history and cultural studies, Google Bard can provide historical facts, timelines, and information about significant events and figures.

```
// Example of a historical query with Google Bard
exploreHistoricalEvent("The American Revolution");
```

8. Encouraging Critical Thinking

Google Bard can facilitate critical thinking by presenting multiple perspectives on a topic. You can ask for different viewpoints and opinions to encourage thoughtful analysis.

```
// Example of seeking different viewpoints with Google Bard
getDifferentOpinions("Pros and cons of renewable energy");
```

9. Interactive Learning

Google Bard's interactive elements, such as knowledge panels and voice responses, can make learning more engaging and interactive, especially for visual or auditory learners.

```
// Example of interactive learning with Google Bard
interactWithKnowledgePanel("Exploring the Solar System"
);
```

10. Collaborative Learning

Educators and students can collaborate and share insights using Google Bard. Collaborative research, group discussions, and knowledge sharing can be enhanced through voice and text interactions.

```
// Example of collaborative learning with Google Bard
collaborateWithPeers("Group discussion on climate chang
e");
```

Google Bard's adaptability and extensive knowledge base make it a valuable tool for educational purposes. Whether you're looking to enhance your understanding of a subject, conduct research, or foster interactive learning experiences, Google Bard can assist in your educational journey.

4.3 Shopping and Consumer Research

Google Bard can be a valuable companion for consumers looking to make informed purchasing decisions. Whether you're shopping for products online or conducting research before making a significant purchase, Google Bard offers features and capabilities that can help you find the best deals, reviews, and product information.

1. Product Research

Before making a purchase, you can use Google Bard to research products. Ask for specifications, features, and user reviews to determine if a product meets your needs.

```
// Example of product research with Google Bard
researchProduct("iPhone 13 Pro Max");
```

2. Price Comparison

Google Bard can assist in comparing prices across different online retailers. This can help you find the best deals and save money.

```
// Example of price comparison with Google Bard
comparePrices("Samsung 4K Smart TV");
```

3. User Reviews

Access user reviews and ratings for products and services. Google Bard can aggregate reviews from multiple sources to provide a comprehensive view of the product's quality.

```
// Example of checking user reviews with Google Bard
getUserReviews("Best noise-canceling headphones");
```

4. Discounts and Deals

Stay informed about discounts, promotions, and deals on various products. Google Bard can provide information on ongoing sales and special offers.

```
// Example of finding discounts with Google Bard
findDiscounts("Laptop deals February 2024");
```

5. Shopping Lists

Create and manage shopping lists using Google Bard. You can add or remove items and even check off completed purchases.

```
// Example of managing a shopping list with Google Bard
createShoppingList("Groceries for the week");
```

6. Local Shopping

For local shopping needs, Google Bard can provide information about nearby stores, their hours of operation, and directions to their locations.

```
// Example of finding local stores with Google Bard
findLocalElectronicsStores("Electronics stores near me"
);
```

7. Product Recommendations

Based on your preferences and previous searches, Google Bard can provide personalized product recommendations, helping you discover new items of interest.

```
// Example of receiving product recommendations with Go
ogle Bard
getPersonalizedRecommendations();
```

8. Delivery Tracking

For online shoppers, Google Bard can track the status of your deliveries and provide real-time updates on package delivery times.

```
// Example of tracking a package with Google Bard
trackPackage("Order #12345");
```

9. Return and Warranty Information

If you have questions about product warranties or return policies, Google Bard can assist in finding relevant information.

```
// Example of checking a product's warranty with Google Bard
checkProductWarranty("Apple Watch Series 7");
```

10. Product Availability

Google Bard can inform you about the availability of specific products in your area or online, helping you make informed decisions about where to purchase.

```
// Example of checking product availability with Google Bard
checkProductAvailability("Nintendo Switch OLED");
```

Google Bard's capabilities make it a versatile tool for shopping and consumer research. Whether you're looking for information about products, searching for the best prices, or managing your shopping lists, Google Bard can simplify the decision-making process and enhance your overall shopping experience.

4.4 Travel Planning and Local Information

Google Bard is a valuable tool for travelers and individuals seeking local information. Whether you're planning a trip or simply exploring your local area, Google Bard provides features and capabilities to help you with travel planning, finding attractions, and getting local insights.

1. Trip Planning

When planning a trip, you can use Google Bard to search for destinations, flights, accommodations, and itineraries. Ask for travel recommendations or information about specific cities or countries.

```
// Example of trip planning with Google Bard
planTrip("Paris travel itinerary");
```

2. Flight and Hotel Reservations

Google Bard can assist in booking flights and accommodations by providing options, prices, and availability. You can also ask about flight status and hotel amenities.

```
// Example of booking a flight with Google Bard
bookFlight("New York to London");
```

3. Local Attractions

Explore local attractions and points of interest with Google Bard. Ask about museums, landmarks, restaurants, and activities in your current location.

```
// Example of finding local attractions with Google Bard
findLocalAttractions("Things to do in San Francisco");
```

4. Dining Recommendations

Looking for a place to eat? Google Bard can recommend restaurants based on your preferences, cuisine, and location.

```
// Example of getting dining recommendations with Google Bard
recommendDining("Italian restaurants in Manhattan");
```

5. Public Transportation

When navigating a new city, Google Bard can provide information about public transportation options, schedules, and routes.

```
// Example of checking public transportation routes with Google Bard
findPublicTransport("Subway directions to Times Square");
```

6. Weather Updates

Stay updated on the weather conditions in your current location or at your travel destination.

```
// Example of checking the weather with Google Bard
checkWeather("Weather forecast for London");
```

7. Currency Conversion

For international travelers, Google Bard can convert currencies and provide exchange rates to help with financial planning.

```
// Example of currency conversion with Google Bard
convertCurrency("USD to Euro");
```

8. Language Assistance

If you're traveling to a foreign country, Google Bard's language translation capabilities can help you communicate and understand the local language.

```
// Example of Language translation for travelers with Google Bard
translateText("Translate 'Hello, how much does this cost?' to French");
```

9. Local Events and Entertainment

Discover local events, concerts, and entertainment options by asking Google Bard for information about what's happening in your area.

```
// Example of finding Local events with Google Bard
findLocalEvents("Concerts in Boston this weekend");
```

10. Emergency Information

In case of emergencies, Google Bard can provide contact information for local authorities, hospitals, and emergency services.

```
// Example of accessing emergency information with Google Bard
emergencyContacts("Emergency numbers in Los Angeles");
```

Google Bard's capabilities make it an excellent companion for travelers and anyone seeking local information. Whether you're planning a vacation, exploring a new city, or simply looking for a nearby restaurant, Google Bard can provide the information you need to make the most of your experience.

4.5 Entertainment and Media Queries

Google Bard offers a wide range of capabilities for entertainment and media-related queries. Whether you're looking for information about movies, music, books, or the latest trends in the entertainment industry, Google Bard can be a valuable resource. In this section, we'll explore how Google Bard can enhance your entertainment and media experiences.

1. Movie and TV Show Information

You can use Google Bard to find information about movies, TV shows, actors, directors, release dates, and ratings. Ask for movie recommendations or details about your favorite films and series.

```
// Example of getting movie information with Google Bard
getMovieInfo("Inception");
```

2. Music Exploration

Discover new music, song lyrics, and artist biographies using Google Bard. You can also ask for music recommendations based on your preferences.

```
// Example of exploring music with Google Bard
exploreMusic("Top songs of 2024");
```

3. Book Recommendations

If you're a book lover, Google Bard can recommend books, provide author information, and offer book summaries. Ask for book recommendations in your favorite genre.

```
// Example of getting book recommendations with Google Bard
recommendBooks("Mystery novels");
```

4. Gaming Information

Stay updated on the gaming world with Google Bard. Get information about video games, gaming consoles, release dates, and gameplay tips.

```
// Example of getting gaming information with Google Bard
getGameInfo("Cyberpunk 2077");
```

5. Sports Updates

Sports enthusiasts can use Google Bard to check scores, schedules, and information about their favorite sports teams and athletes.

```
// Example of checking sports scores with Google Bard
checkSportsScores("New York Yankees");
```

6. Event Tickets

When you're interested in attending concerts, sports events, or theater shows, Google Bard can help you find tickets, event details, and seating information.

```
// Example of finding event tickets with Google Bard
findConcertTickets("Taylor Swift concert tickets");
```

7. News and Celebrity Gossip

Stay informed about the latest entertainment news, celebrity gossip, and trends in the entertainment industry.

```
// Example of getting entertainment news with Google Bard
getEntertainmentNews("Hollywood celebrity updates");
```

8. Movie and Music Recommendations

Google Bard can recommend movies, TV shows, songs, and albums based on your preferences and viewing or listening history.

```
// Example of receiving movie recommendations with Goog
le Bard
getMovieRecommendations();
```

9. Gaming Tips and Strategies

Gamers can seek gaming tips, strategies, and cheat codes for various video games to enhance their gaming experience.

```
// Example of getting gaming tips with Google Bard
getGamingTips("Fortnite building strategies");
```

10. Media Streaming

Ask Google Bard to play your favorite songs, albums, podcasts, or radio stations using integrated media streaming services.

```
// Example of playing music with Google Bard
playMusic("Play 'Bohemian Rhapsody' by Queen");
```

Google Bard's entertainment and media capabilities make it a versatile companion for those looking to stay entertained, discover new content, or stay informed about the latest trends in the entertainment industry. Whether you're a movie buff, music enthusiast, bookworm, or sports fan, Google Bard has something to offer for everyone in the world of entertainment and media.

Chapter 5: Business Applications of Google Bard

5.1 Market Research and Data Analysis

Google Bard can be a powerful tool for businesses seeking to gather insights, analyze data, and stay competitive in their respective markets. In this section, we'll explore how Google Bard can be applied to market research and data analysis, providing businesses with valuable information to make informed decisions.

1. Competitive Analysis

One of the key aspects of market research is understanding the competitive landscape. Google Bard can assist in gathering data on competitors, including their products, pricing, marketing strategies, and customer reviews.

```
// Example of competitive analysis with Google Bard
analyzeCompetitors("Top competitors in the smartphone industry");
```

2. Industry Trends and Insights

Stay up-to-date with industry trends and emerging technologies. Google Bard can provide information on the latest trends, innovations, and market dynamics in your industry.

```
// Example of staying informed about industry trends with Google Bard
industryTrends("Artificial intelligence trends in healthcare");
```

3. Customer Feedback Analysis

Analyze customer feedback and reviews to gain insights into product satisfaction, identify areas for improvement, and monitor customer sentiment.

```
// Example of analyzing customer feedback with Google Bard
```

```
analyzeCustomerReviews("Product reviews for XYZ Corpora
tion");
```

4. Data Visualization

Google Bard can assist in generating charts, graphs, and data visualizations to make complex data more understandable for business stakeholders.

```
// Example of creating a data visualization with Google
Bard
generateDataVisualization("Sales performance over the l
ast year");
```

5. Market Surveys and Research

Conduct market surveys and research by using Google Bard to gather data on consumer preferences, behaviors, and demographics.

```
// Example of conducting a market survey with Google Ba
rd
conductMarketSurvey("Consumer preferences for eco-frien
dly products");
```

6. Pricing Strategy

Determine optimal pricing strategies by analyzing pricing data and competitor pricing models to maximize profitability.

```
// Example of pricing strategy analysis with Google Bar
d
optimizePricingStrategy("Dynamic pricing for e-commerce
");
```

7. Sales Forecasting

Google Bard can assist in forecasting sales by analyzing historical sales data, market trends, and seasonality.

```
// Example of sales forecasting with Google Bard
forecastSales("Sales projections for Q3 2024");
```

8. Product Development Insights

Use Google Bard to gather insights for product development, including feature requests, market gaps, and customer needs.

```
// Example of gathering insights for product developmen
t with Google Bard
productDevelopmentInsights("Features requested by custo
mers for our software");
```

9. Brand Reputation Monitoring

Monitor your brand's online reputation by analyzing social media mentions, reviews, and news articles to address any potential PR issues.

```
// Example of brand reputation monitoring with Google B
ard
monitorBrandReputation("Online mentions of our brand");
```

10. Investment and Market Entry Analysis

Businesses looking to expand or invest in new markets can use Google Bard to gather data on market entry strategies, investment opportunities, and potential risks.

```
// Example of market entry analysis with Google Bard
analyzeMarketEntryOpportunities("Entering the South Ame
rican market");
```

Google Bard's capabilities in market research and data analysis make it a valuable asset for businesses seeking to gain a competitive edge, make data-driven decisions, and stay informed about market dynamics. Whether you're a startup or an established enterprise, Google Bard can assist in various aspects of business intelligence and market research.

5.2 Enhancing SEO and Digital Marketing

Google Bard plays a significant role in enhancing Search Engine Optimization (SEO) and digital marketing strategies for businesses. SEO is crucial for improving a website's visibility on search engines, and Google Bard can provide valuable insights and tools to optimize your online presence. In this section, we'll explore how Google Bard can be used to enhance SEO and digital marketing efforts.

1. Keyword Research

Keyword research is the foundation of SEO. Google Bard can help you identify relevant keywords and search queries that users are using to find products or services similar to yours.

```
// Example of keyword research with Google Bard
performKeywordResearch("Best SEO tools for small businesses");
```

2. Content Optimization

Optimizing website content for search engines is vital. Google Bard can provide recommendations for improving content, including keyword placement, readability, and structure.

```
// Example of content optimization tips from Google Bard
optimizeContent("How to write SEO-friendly blog posts");
```

3. Backlink Analysis

Backlinks are essential for SEO, and Google Bard can assist in analyzing backlink profiles, identifying quality backlinks, and finding opportunities for link building.

```
// Example of backlink analysis with Google Bard
analyzeBacklinkProfile("Backlinks for my website");
```

4. Competitor Analysis

Competitor analysis is crucial to understand what works in your industry. Google Bard can provide insights into your competitors' SEO strategies, keywords, and ranking positions.

```
// Example of competitor analysis with Google Bard
analyzeCompetitorSEO("Competitor analysis for e-commerce");
```

5. SEO Audits

Regular SEO audits are essential to identify issues and improvements on your website. Google Bard can provide guidelines for conducting SEO audits and fixing common SEO issues.

```
// Example of conducting an SEO audit with Google Bard
performSEOAudit("Website SEO audit checklist");
```

6. Local SEO

For businesses targeting local customers, Google Bard can help optimize your local SEO efforts by providing tips for optimizing Google My Business profiles and local search visibility.

```
// Example of optimizing local SEO with Google Bard
localSEOOptimization("Improving local search rankings");
```

7. Content Marketing Ideas

Google Bard can provide content marketing ideas and topic suggestions based on trending topics and user interests.

```
// Example of content marketing ideas from Google Bard
generateContentIdeas("Content ideas for a fashion blog");
```

8. Social Media Strategies

Social media plays a significant role in digital marketing. Google Bard can offer advice on social media strategies, content calendars, and engagement tactics.

```
// Example of social media strategy tips from Google Bard
socialMediaStrategy("Effective social media posting schedule");
```

9. Paid Advertising Guidance

If you're running paid advertising campaigns, Google Bard can provide insights into optimizing ad copy, targeting options, and budget allocation.

```
// Example of paid advertising guidance from Google Bard
optimizeAdCampaign("Improving Google Ads ROI");
```

10. Performance Tracking

Track your SEO and digital marketing performance with Google Bard. Receive reports on website traffic, keyword rankings, and conversion rates.

```
// Example of performance tracking with Google Bard
trackDigitalMarketingPerformance("Monthly SEO performance report");
```

Google Bard's capabilities make it a valuable resource for businesses aiming to improve their SEO and digital marketing strategies. Whether you're a small business owner or a digital marketing professional, Google Bard can provide insights, tips, and recommendations to help you enhance your online presence and reach your target audience more effectively.

5.3 Customer Service and Engagement

Google Bard can be a valuable asset for improving customer service and engagement for businesses. Providing excellent customer service is essential for building and retaining a loyal customer base. In this section, we'll explore how Google Bard can enhance customer service and engagement strategies.

1. Instant Customer Support

Google Bard can be integrated into your website or app to provide instant customer support. Users can ask questions, report issues, or seek assistance 24/7.

```
// Example of implementing instant customer support wit
h Google Bard
instantCustomerSupport("How can I return a product?");
```

2. FAQ Automation

Automate frequently asked questions (FAQs) using Google Bard. It can answer common queries and provide solutions, reducing the workload on customer support teams.

```
// Example of FAQ automation with Google Bard
automateFAQs("FAQs about account registration");
```

3. Product Recommendations

Use Google Bard to recommend products or services to customers based on their preferences and purchase history.

```
// Example of providing product recommendations with Go
ogle Bard
recommendProducts("Recommended accessories for your sma
rtphone");
```

4. Order Status Updates

Customers can check the status of their orders in real-time by interacting with Google Bard, reducing the need for them to contact customer support.

```
// Example of checking order status with Google Bard
checkOrderStatus("Where is my order #12345?");
```

5. Troubleshooting Assistance

Google Bard can assist customers in troubleshooting common issues with products or services, providing step-by-step solutions.

```
// Example of troubleshooting assistance with Google Bard
troubleshootIssues("How to fix a slow internet connection");
```

6. Appointment Scheduling

For businesses offering services by appointment, customers can use Google Bard to schedule appointments, check availability, and receive confirmations.

```
// Example of appointment scheduling with Google Bard
scheduleAppointment("Book a dental check-up for next week");
```

7. Feedback Collection

Gather feedback and suggestions from customers using Google Bard's survey and feedback collection capabilities.

```
// Example of collecting feedback with Google Bard
collectCustomerFeedback("How would you rate your shopping experience?");
```

8. Product Knowledge Base

Google Bard can provide access to a comprehensive product knowledge base, helping customers find answers to their questions independently.

```
// Example of accessing a product knowledge base with Google Bard
accessProductKnowledgeBase("User manual for XYZ product");
```

9. Loyalty Programs and Rewards

Engage customers with loyalty programs and rewards by using Google Bard to provide information on available perks and promotions.

```
// Example of loyalty program information with Google Bard
loyaltyProgramInfo("Benefits of joining our loyalty program");
```

10. Follow-Up and Surveys

After a customer interaction, Google Bard can send follow-up messages and surveys to gather feedback and ensure customer satisfaction.

```
// Example of sending a follow-up survey with Google Bard
sendFollowUpSurvey("Did our support team resolve your issue?");
```

Google Bard's capabilities can significantly improve customer service and engagement, leading to higher customer satisfaction and loyalty. Whether you're a small business or a large corporation, integrating Google Bard into your customer support and engagement strategies can help you provide a seamless and responsive customer experience.

5.4 Competitive Analysis

Competitive analysis is a critical component of business strategy, and Google Bard can provide valuable insights to help businesses gain a competitive edge. Understanding your competitors, their strengths, weaknesses, and market positioning can guide your decision-making and help you identify opportunities for growth. In this section, we'll explore how Google Bard can assist in competitive analysis.

1. Competitor Identification

Google Bard can help you identify your key competitors in the industry by analyzing search results, market reports, and online mentions.

```
// Example of competitor identification with Google Bard
identifyCompetitors("Who are the top competitors in the software industry?");
```

2. SWOT Analysis

Conduct a SWOT analysis (Strengths, Weaknesses, Opportunities, Threats) of your competitors with Google Bard's assistance. It can provide insights into their internal and external factors.

```
// Example of conducting a SWOT analysis with Google Bard
swotAnalysis("SWOT analysis of Company XYZ");
```

3. Market Share and Positioning

Determine your competitors' market share and positioning within the industry. Google Bard can provide data on market rankings and shares.

```
// Example of analyzing market share with Google Bard
marketShareAnalysis("Market share of leading smartphone manufacturers");
```

4. Product and Service Offerings

Explore your competitors' product and service offerings, including features, pricing, and customer reviews.

```
// Example of analyzing product offerings with Google Bard
analyzeProductOfferings("Product comparison of top e-commerce platforms");
```

5. Pricing Strategies

Understand your competitors' pricing strategies, including discounts, promotions, and pricing models.

```
// Example of analyzing pricing strategies with Google Bard
pricingStrategyAnalysis("Competitors' pricing for streaming services");
```

6. Customer Reviews and Feedback

Gather insights from customer reviews and feedback on your competitors' products or services to identify areas for improvement.

```
// Example of analyzing customer reviews with Google Bard
analyzeCustomerFeedback("Customer reviews of competing fitness trackers");
```

7. Marketing and Advertising Analysis

Examine your competitors' marketing and advertising efforts, including ad campaigns, social media presence, and content strategies.

```
// Example of analyzing marketing efforts with Google Bard
marketingAnalysis("Competitors' social media advertising campaigns");
```

8. Innovation and Research

Stay informed about your competitors' innovation efforts and research initiatives by analyzing news articles and reports.

```
// Example of monitoring competitors' innovation with Google Bard
innovationMonitoring("Latest innovations in the automotive industry");
```

9. Online Presence and SEO

Evaluate your competitors' online presence and SEO strategies to understand how they drive traffic and engagement.

```
// Example of analyzing competitors' online presence wi
th Google Bard
onlinePresenceAnalysis("Competitors' website traffic an
d SEO performance");
```

10. Benchmarking and Strategy Development

Utilize the insights gained from competitive analysis to benchmark your business against competitors and develop informed strategies.

```
// Example of strategy development based on competitive
analysis with Google Bard
developCompetitiveStrategy("Strategies to outperform co
mpetitors in the fashion industry");
```

Google Bard's capabilities in competitive analysis can provide businesses with a comprehensive understanding of their competitive landscape. By leveraging the insights and data provided, businesses can make informed decisions, refine their strategies, and ultimately strive for a stronger market position and growth. Whether you're a startup or an established enterprise, competitive analysis is essential for staying competitive in today's dynamic business environment.

5.5 Trends Forecasting and Industry Insights

Trends forecasting and gaining industry insights are essential for businesses to adapt, innovate, and remain competitive. Google Bard can play a significant role in helping businesses anticipate trends, identify emerging opportunities, and stay informed about industry developments. In this section, we'll explore how Google

Bard can assist in trends forecasting and providing valuable industry insights.

1. Trend Analysis

Google Bard can analyze data from various sources to identify emerging trends in your industry, whether it's technology, fashion, healthcare, or any other sector.

```
// Example of trend analysis with Google Bard
analyzeIndustryTrends("Emerging trends in sustainable fashion");
```

2. Consumer Behavior Insights

Understand changing consumer behaviors and preferences by analyzing online discussions, surveys, and social media trends.

```
// Example of gaining consumer behavior insights with Google Bard
consumerBehaviorAnalysis("Shifting preferences in online shopping");
```

3. Market Research Reports

Access market research reports, industry studies, and market forecasts to make informed decisions about your business strategies.

```
// Example of accessing market research reports with Google Bard
accessMarketResearch("Market forecast for electric vehicles");
```

4. Technology Trends

Stay updated on the latest technology trends, innovations, and breakthroughs that could impact your industry.

```
// Example of staying informed about technology trends with Google Bard
technologyTrends("Recent advancements in artificial intelligence");
```

5. Competitive Intelligence

Google Bard can provide insights into your competitors' strategies, product launches, and market moves to help you adapt and stay competitive.

```
// Example of competitive intelligence gathering with Google Bard
gatherCompetitiveIntelligence("Competitor product launches in the smartphone industry");
```

6. Regulatory Changes

Stay informed about changes in regulations and compliance standards that may affect your industry and business operations.

```
// Example of monitoring regulatory changes with Google Bard
regulatoryChanges("Updates in data privacy regulations");
```

7. Global Market Insights

Access insights into global markets, trade trends, and economic conditions to make informed decisions about international expansion.

```
// Example of gaining global market insights with Google Bard
globalMarketInsights("Market opportunities in the Asia-Pacific region");
```

8. Industry Events and Conferences

Stay updated on industry events, conferences, and trade shows to network and gain insights from thought leaders.

```
// Example of accessing information on industry events with Google Bard
industryEvents("Upcoming healthcare conferences in 2024");
```

9. Investment Opportunities

Google Bard can provide information on potential investment opportunities, startups, and emerging players in your industry.

```
// Example of exploring investment opportunities with G
oogle Bard
exploreInvestmentOpportunities("Promising startups in r
enewable energy");
```

10. Predictive Analytics

Leverage predictive analytics with Google Bard to anticipate future market conditions and customer behavior patterns.

```
// Example of using predictive analytics with Google Ba
rd
predictMarketTrends("Predicting e-commerce trends for t
he next year");
```

Google Bard's capabilities in trends forecasting and industry insights provide businesses with a competitive advantage by helping them stay ahead of the curve. Whether you're an entrepreneur, business executive, or industry professional, harnessing the power of Google Bard can assist in making informed decisions, seizing opportunities, and thriving in an ever-evolving business landscape.

Chapter 6: Understanding AI and Natural Language Processing

Chapter 6: Understanding AI and Natural Language Processing

6.1 The Basics of AI in Search Engines

Artificial Intelligence (AI) has transformed the landscape of search engines, and understanding its basics is crucial to grasp how Google Bard operates. In this section, we'll delve into the fundamental concepts of AI in search engines and how it has revolutionized information retrieval.

1. What is Artificial Intelligence?

Artificial Intelligence refers to the development of computer systems capable of performing tasks that typically require human intelligence. These tasks include problem-solving, learning, reasoning, understanding natural language, and more.

```
# Example of AI in action: Natural Language Understanding
text = "Translate this English sentence to French."
translated_text = translate(text, source_language='en', target_language='fr')
```

2. The Role of AI in Search Engines

In traditional search engines, queries were matched with keywords, and results were ranked based on their relevance. AI has enhanced this process by understanding the context and intent behind the queries.

```
# Traditional search engine query
query = "Apple"
results = traditionalSearch(query)


# AI-powered search engine query
query = "Tell me about Apple Inc."
results = aiPoweredSearch(query)
```

3. Machine Learning and Search Ranking

AI-driven search engines use Machine Learning algorithms to improve search ranking. They analyze user behavior and feedback to fine-tune the results, providing more relevant and personalized content.

```
# Machine Learning in search ranking
user_feedback = {"clicked_result": 1, "not_relevant": 3
}
updateSearchRanking(user_feedback)
```

4. Natural Language Processing (NLP)

NLP is a subset of AI that focuses on enabling computers to understand, interpret, and generate human language. Google Bard utilizes NLP to comprehend and respond to natural language queries.

```
# NLP for natural language queries
user_query = "What's the weather like today?"
response = nlpProcess(user_query)
```

5. Conversational AI

Conversational AI, like voice assistants and chatbots, relies heavily on AI and NLP to engage in human-like conversations. Google Bard's voice search feature is an example of conversational AI.

```
# Conversational AI interaction
user_input = voiceInput()
response = chatbotResponse(user_input)
```

6. AI in Understanding User Intent

One of the most significant AI advancements in search is the ability to understand user intent. AI-driven search engines decipher what users want, even if the query is vague or complex.

```
# AI understanding user intent
user_query = "Where can I find Italian restaurants near
```

```
by?"
understood_intent = aiUnderstandIntent(user_query)
```

7. Future Possibilities with AI

AI continues to evolve, and its integration into search engines opens up possibilities for more accurate, efficient, and personalized information retrieval. It also raises important questions about ethics and responsible AI use.

```
# Future AI possibilities
future_ai_features = ["Enhanced personalization", "Real
-time language translation", "Context-aware recommendat
ions"]
```

Understanding the basics of AI in search engines is a stepping stone to harnessing the full potential of Google Bard and similar AI-powered search technologies. As AI continues to advance, it will shape the future of information access and user experiences in unprecedented ways.

6.2 How Google Bard Processes Language

Understanding how Google Bard processes language is essential to grasp its capabilities in interpreting and responding to user queries. In this section, we'll explore the intricate process of language processing within Google Bard.

1. Text Tokenization

Text tokenization is the process of breaking down a text into individual words or tokens. Google Bard utilizes tokenization to analyze the structure of user queries and text documents.

```
# Text tokenization in Google Bard
text = "What are the benefits of AI in healthcare?"
tokens = tokenize(text)
```

2. Part-of-Speech Tagging

Part-of-speech tagging assigns grammatical categories to each token in a sentence, such as nouns, verbs, adjectives, etc. This helps Google Bard understand the role of each word in a query.

```
# Part-of-speech tagging in language processing
sentence = "The quick brown fox jumps over the lazy dog."
pos_tags = posTag(sentence)
```

3. Named Entity Recognition (NER)

NER identifies and classifies named entities in text, such as names of people, organizations, locations, and more. Google Bard uses NER to extract relevant information from queries.

```
# Named Entity Recognition in Google Bard
text = "Tell me about Apple Inc."
named_entities = recognizeEntities(text)
```

4. Dependency Parsing

Dependency parsing determines the grammatical relationships between words in a sentence. It helps Google Bard understand the syntactic structure of a query.

```
# Dependency parsing in language processing
sentence = "The cat chased the mouse."
dependency_tree = parseDependencies(sentence)
```

5. Sentiment Analysis

Sentiment analysis evaluates the sentiment or emotion expressed in a piece of text, whether it's positive, negative, or neutral. Google Bard can use sentiment analysis to gauge user sentiment in queries.

```
# Sentiment analysis in Google Bard
user_feedback = "I love this product! It's amazing."
sentiment = analyzeSentiment(user_feedback)
```

6. Language Translation

Google Bard can translate text between different languages using machine translation models. This feature is useful for providing information in multiple languages.

```
# Language translation in Google Bard
text = "Translate this English text to Spanish."
translated_text = translate(text, source_language='en', target_language='es')
```

7. Question Answering

Google Bard's language processing capabilities enable it to understand and answer questions posed in natural language. It extracts information from various sources to provide relevant answers.

```
# Question answering with Google Bard
question = "Who is the CEO of Google?"
answer = answerQuestion(question)
```

8. Contextual Understanding

Contextual understanding is a key aspect of Google Bard's language processing. It considers the context of a conversation or query to provide more accurate responses.

```
# Contextual understanding in conversation
user_input = "What's the weather like today?"
context = "Location: New York"
response = contextualResponse(user_input, context)
```

9. Multilingual Support

Google Bard's language processing capabilities extend to multiple languages, allowing users to interact with the AI in their preferred language.

```
# Multilingual support in Google Bard
user_query = "Quels sont les restaurants français à Paris?"
response = processQuery(user_query, language='fr')
```

10. Continuous Learning

Google Bard's language processing models are continually updated and trained on new data to improve accuracy and keep up with language evolution.

```
# Continuous learning and model updates
model_update = updateLanguageModel()
```

Understanding how Google Bard processes language provides insights into its ability to comprehend and respond effectively to user queries. This sophisticated language processing underpins its role in delivering relevant and context-aware information to users across a wide range of topics and languages.

6.3 The Role of Machine Learning

Machine Learning (ML) plays a pivotal role in Google Bard's ability to process and understand user queries, enabling it to provide relevant and context-aware responses. In this section, we'll explore the significance of ML in Google Bard's operations.

1. Training Data

At the heart of Google Bard's ML algorithms lies extensive training data. These datasets include a wide variety of text documents, user queries, and interactions, which the system uses to learn patterns and associations.

```
# Training data collection for Google Bard
train_data = gatherTrainingData()
```

2. Natural Language Understanding

ML models in Google Bard are trained to understand natural language. They can recognize synonyms, context, and even nuances in user queries, making it possible to respond effectively.

```
# ML-based natural language understanding
user_query = "Find Italian restaurants nearby."
response = mlUnderstandQuery(user_query)
```

3. Personalization

Machine Learning allows Google Bard to personalize search results and recommendations based on user behavior and preferences. It adapts to individual users over time, providing a tailored experience.

```
# Personalization with ML
user_profile = getUserProfile()
personalized_results = personalizeResults(user_profile)
```

4. Search Ranking

ML algorithms are used to rank search results based on relevance and user engagement. Google Bard continuously refines its ranking models to ensure users receive the most valuable information.

```
# ML-driven search ranking
user_feedback = {"clicked_result": 1, "not_relevant": 3
}
updateSearchRanking(user_feedback)
```

5. User Intent Prediction

ML models excel in predicting user intent. Google Bard uses historical query data to anticipate what users are looking for, even when queries are vague or incomplete.

```
# ML-based user intent prediction
user_query = "Tell me about the latest smartphones."
predicted_intent = predictUserIntent(user_query)
```

6. Contextual Understanding

Machine Learning helps Google Bard understand context within conversations or queries. This context-awareness is essential for providing meaningful responses.

```
# ML-based contextual understanding
user_input = "What's the weather like today?"
context = "Location: San Francisco"
response = contextualResponse(user_input, context)
```

7. Continuous Improvement

ML models are not static; they continuously learn and adapt. Google Bard's ML algorithms are regularly updated to stay relevant and accurate.

```
# Continuous improvement of ML models
model_update = updateMachineLearningModel()
```

8. Data Privacy

Google Bard also employs ML to protect user data and ensure privacy. It uses anonymization and encryption techniques to safeguard sensitive information.

```
# Data privacy measures with ML
user_data = encryptUserData(user_profile)
```

9. Multilingual Capabilities

Machine Learning enables Google Bard to support multiple languages effectively. ML models can be fine-tuned for each language, allowing users to interact in their preferred language.

```
# Multilingual support with ML
user_query = "¿Dónde está la estación de tren más cercana?"
response = mlProcessQuery(user_query, language='es')
```

10. Future Developments

As Machine Learning continues to advance, Google Bard's capabilities will evolve as well. It will lead to more accurate, efficient, and personalized responses, enhancing the overall user experience.

Machine Learning is at the core of Google Bard's ability to comprehend user queries, adapt to user preferences, and deliver meaningful results. Its dynamic nature ensures that Google Bard remains a cutting-edge AI-powered search engine that continually improves its performance.

6.4 AI Ethics and Responsible Use

In the realm of AI and machine learning, ethics and responsible use are paramount. Google Bard, as a powerful AI-driven search engine, operates within a framework of ethical considerations and guidelines. This section delves into the importance of AI ethics and responsible usage in the context of Google Bard.

1. Fairness and Bias Mitigation

AI systems like Google Bard are susceptible to biases present in training data. It's crucial to actively mitigate biases to ensure fair treatment of all users and to provide unbiased search results.

```
# Fairness and bias mitigation in AI
checkForBias(data)
applyBiasMitigationTechniques(model)
```

2. Transparency

Transparency is vital in AI systems. Google Bard aims to provide users with transparency about how it processes queries, collects data, and makes decisions.

```
# Transparency in AI operations
explainModelDecisions(model)
discloseDataCollectionPolicies()
```

3. Privacy by Design

Google Bard follows a privacy-by-design approach, incorporating privacy considerations into its development from the beginning. User data is handled with care and in compliance with privacy regulations.

```
# Privacy by design principles
implementDataAnonymization()
encryptUserData()
```

4. User Consent

User consent is a fundamental aspect of responsible AI usage. Google Bard seeks explicit user consent for data collection and personalization features.

```
# Obtaining user consent in AI applications
requestUserConsent()
handleUserDataPreferences()
```

5. Data Security

AI systems must prioritize data security. Google Bard employs encryption and secure data storage practices to protect user information.

```
# Data security measures in AI
secureDataStorage()
regularlyAuditDataAccess()
```

6. Accountability and Governance

Clear accountability and governance structures are in place to ensure that responsible AI practices are upheld. Google Bard has dedicated teams responsible for ethical AI development and oversight.

```
# Accountability and governance in AI
establishEthicsReviewBoard()
conductRegularEthicalAudits()
```

7. Addressing Ethical Dilemmas

AI systems may encounter ethical dilemmas. Google Bard is programmed to handle such situations with caution, prioritizing user well-being and ethical principles.

```
# Addressing ethical dilemmas in AI
ethicalDecisionMaking()
ethicalFallbackResponses()
```

8. User Education

Google Bard provides users with information about responsible AI use and encourages them to be aware of ethical considerations when interacting with the system.

```
# User education on AI ethics
provideEthicalGuidelines()
offerUserEducationResources()
```

9. Continuous Monitoring and Improvement

Google Bard continually monitors its operations for ethical compliance and seeks ways to improve its ethical practices.

```
# Continuous monitoring and improvement of AI ethics
conductEthicalImpactAssessments()
implementEthicalFeedbackLoops()
```

10. Ethical AI Community

Google Bard actively participates in the broader AI ethics community, collaborating with experts, researchers, and organizations to contribute to the development of ethical AI standards and best practices.

```
# Collaboration with the AI ethics community
engageInEthicalAIResearch()
participateInEthicalAIConferences()
```

In conclusion, Google Bard places a strong emphasis on AI ethics and responsible use. These principles are deeply embedded in its design, development, and operation to ensure that it serves users in a fair, transparent, and privacy-conscious manner. The continuous commitment to ethical AI reflects Google Bard's dedication to responsible technology that benefits all.

6.5 Limitations and Challenges of AI in Search

While AI, including Google Bard, has made remarkable advancements in the field of search technology, it is essential to acknowledge its limitations and the challenges it faces. In this section, we will explore some of the key constraints and obstacles that AI-powered search engines like Google Bard encounter.

1. Data Dependence

AI search engines heavily rely on data. The quality and quantity of available data directly impact their performance. In niche or less-documented areas, the lack of sufficient data can hinder accurate search results.

```
# Data dependency in AI search
checkDataAvailability()
dataAugmentationTechniques()
```

2. Biased Training Data

Bias present in training data can lead to biased search results. AI models may inadvertently reinforce existing biases, making it crucial to address and mitigate bias in AI systems.

```
# Addressing bias in AI training data
detectBiasInData()
implementBiasMitigationStrategies()
```

3. Ethical Dilemmas

AI search engines may encounter ethical dilemmas, such as prioritizing information accuracy over user preferences. Balancing these dilemmas is a complex challenge.

```
# Handling ethical dilemmas in AI search
ethicalDecisionMaking()
UserPreferenceVsAccuracy()
```

4. Contextual Understanding

Understanding context is challenging for AI. Ambiguity in user queries and the need to grasp the broader context of a conversation remain areas of improvement.

```
# Enhancing contextual understanding in AI
contextualQueryInterpretation()
contextualResponseGeneration()
```

5. Personalization Balance

While personalization enhances user experience, it can lead to filter bubbles and limit exposure to diverse perspectives. Striking the right balance between personalization and diversity is a challenge.

```
# Balancing personalization and diversity in AI search
evaluatePersonalizationEffects()
recommendDiverseContent()
```

6. Scalability

Scalability is crucial for AI search engines to handle a vast amount of user queries. Scaling AI models while maintaining efficiency is an ongoing challenge.

```
# Achieving scalability in AI search
optimizeModelSize()
parallelProcessingTechniques()
```

7. User Privacy

AI search engines must respect user privacy. Striking a balance between personalization and privacy can be complex, requiring robust data protection measures.

```
# Balancing user privacy and personalization in AI
implementPrivacyByDesign()
offerPrivacySettings()
```

8. Misinformation and Disinformation

AI search engines face the challenge of identifying and mitigating misinformation and disinformation in search results, contributing to a trustworthy information ecosystem.

```
# Detecting and addressing misinformation in AI search
developMisinformationDetectionModels()
factCheckIntegration()
```

9. User Interface Design

Designing an intuitive user interface that effectively communicates AI capabilities and limitations is crucial for user satisfaction and trust.

```
# User interface design considerations for AI search
userInterfaceFeedbackLoop()
clearLimitationCommunication()
```

10. Evolving Technology

The field of AI and search technology is continuously evolving. Keeping AI systems up to date with the latest advancements is essential for maintaining their effectiveness.

```
# Adapting AI search to evolving technology
monitorAIAdvancements()
regularModelUpdates()
```

In summary, AI search engines like Google Bard bring immense value, but they are not without their challenges and limitations. Addressing these constraints and continually striving for improvements is essential to ensure that AI-powered search engines remain valuable tools for users while maintaining ethical and responsible practices. The ongoing evolution of AI and search technology will continue to shape the landscape of information retrieval.

Chapter 7: Google Bard for Content Creators

7.1 Researching and Generating Ideas

Content creators, whether they are writers, bloggers, video producers, or social media influencers, often rely on extensive research and creative idea generation to produce engaging and valuable content. Google Bard offers a wide range of tools and techniques that can assist content creators in their research and idea generation processes.

1. Comprehensive Information Retrieval

Google Bard's powerful search capabilities enable content creators to access a vast pool of information quickly. Whether you need background information for an article or data to support your video script, Google Bard can retrieve relevant content efficiently.

```
# Conducting comprehensive information retrieval
searchForContentIdeas(query)
analyzeSearchResults()
```

2. Trend Analysis

Keeping up with the latest trends is crucial for content creators. Google Bard allows you to explore trending topics, keywords, and search queries to align your content with current interests and demands.

```
# Analyzing trends for content ideas
trackTrendingTopics()
keywordAnalysisTools()
```

3. Exploring Niche Topics

For niche content creators, finding information about specialized subjects can be challenging. Google Bard can help you discover niche forums, communities, and sources to gather insights and data for your content.

```
# Exploring niche topics and communities
identifyNicheForums()
searchSpecializedDatabases()
```

4. Competitive Analysis

Understanding what your competitors are doing can be valuable. Google Bard allows you to analyze competitor content, keywords, and strategies to refine your own content creation approach.

```
# Conducting competitive analysis
examineCompetitorContent()
evaluateKeyword Competition()
```

5. Idea Generation Techniques

Stuck in a creative rut? Google Bard offers techniques for idea generation, such as exploring related topics, brainstorming sessions, and content prompts to inspire your next piece of content.

```
# Techniques for generating content ideas
useRelatedSearches()
organizeBrainstormingSessions()
```

6. Data Visualization Tools

For content creators who rely on data-driven content, Google Bard can help you find data sources and visualization tools to create compelling charts, graphs, and infographics.

```
# Data visualization resources
locateDataSources()
selectVisualizationTools()
```

7. Content Validation

Before publishing, it's essential to validate the accuracy of the information you've gathered. Google Bard can assist in fact-checking and verifying the credibility of sources.

```
# Validating content accuracy
conductFactChecking()
evaluateSourceCredibility()
```

8. Collaboration and Sharing

Collaboration is often a part of content creation. Google Bard enables content creators to share their findings and collaborate with team members or fellow creators easily.

```
# Collaboration tools for content creators
collaborateOnResearch()
shareContentIdeas()
```

9. Ethical Content Creation

Ethical considerations are crucial in content creation. Google Bard can provide guidelines and resources to ensure that your content adheres to ethical standards.

```
# Ethical content creation principles
followContentEthics()
accessEthicalGuidelines()
```

10. Continuous Learning

The world of content creation is ever-evolving. Google Bard encourages content creators to engage in continuous learning, offering access to online courses, webinars, and educational resources.

```
# Continuous learning for content creators
enrollInOnlineCourses()
attendContentCreationWebinars()
```

In conclusion, Google Bard is a valuable tool for content creators seeking to research and generate ideas for their projects. Whether you're a professional writer, a YouTuber, or a social media influencer, leveraging the capabilities of Google Bard can enhance your content creation process and help you produce high-quality, informative, and engaging content for your audience.

7.2 Analyzing Audience Trends

Understanding your audience is a crucial aspect of content creation. Google Bard provides content creators with tools and insights to analyze audience trends, preferences, and behaviors. By harnessing these capabilities, content creators can tailor their content to better resonate with their target audience.

1. Audience Segmentation

Google Bard allows content creators to segment their audience based on various factors, including demographics, interests, and location. This segmentation helps creators understand the diversity within their audience and create content that appeals to different segments.

```
# Segmenting the audience for content analysis
segmentByDemographics()
analyzeInterests()
```

2. Content Engagement Metrics

Measuring the performance of your content is essential. Google Bard offers metrics and analytics tools to track engagement, such as views, likes, shares, and comments. These insights help content creators assess the impact of their content.

```
# Tracking content engagement metrics
monitorViews()
analyzeLikesAndShares()
evaluateCommentFeedback()
```

3. Keyword Analysis

Keywords play a significant role in content discovery. Google Bard provides keyword analysis tools that help content creators identify relevant keywords and phrases that their audience is searching for.

```
# Analyzing keywords for content optimization
conductKeywordResearch()
optimizeContentKeywords()
```

4. Social Media Monitoring

Many content creators share their work on social media platforms. Google Bard enables monitoring of social media mentions, hashtags, and trends related to your content or niche.

```
# Monitoring social media trends and mentions
trackHashtags()
analyzeSocialMediaActivity()
```

5. Audience Surveys and Feedback

Gathering direct feedback from your audience is invaluable. Google Bard facilitates the creation of surveys and feedback forms, allowing content creators to collect insights and preferences directly from their audience.

```
# Conducting audience surveys and feedback collection
createAudienceSurveys()
analyzeSurveyResponses()
```

6. Competitive Analysis

Analyzing the content strategies of competitors can provide valuable insights. Google Bard assists content creators in evaluating the content produced by competitors and understanding what resonates with their respective audiences.

```
# Conducting competitive content analysis
evaluateCompetitorContent()
identifyContentGaps()
```

7. Content Personalization

Personalizing content for different audience segments can enhance engagement. Google Bard offers personalization tools to deliver tailored content recommendations based on user preferences.

```
# Personalizing content recommendations
implementPersonalizationStrategies()
trackUserPreferences()
```

8. Content Testing

A/B testing and experimentation are essential for optimizing content. Google Bard provides guidance on how to conduct content tests to determine what resonates best with your audience.

```
# Conducting A/B tests for content optimization
designContentExperiments()
analyzeTestResults()
```

9. Feedback Integration

Integrating audience feedback into your content creation process is crucial. Google Bard offers strategies for incorporating audience suggestions and addressing their concerns effectively.

```
# Integrating audience feedback into content improvement
incorporateAudienceSuggestions()
resolveConcernsConstructively()
```

10. Content Evolution

Audience trends and preferences change over time. Google Bard emphasizes the importance of adapting your content strategy continuously to stay aligned with your audience's evolving interests.

```
# Adapting content strategy to evolving audience trends
monitorAudienceTrends()
evolveContentCreationApproach()
```

In conclusion, Google Bard equips content creators with a wide range of tools and insights to analyze audience trends effectively. By leveraging these resources, content creators can refine their content strategies, produce content that resonates with their audience, and foster stronger connections with their viewers, readers, or followers. Understanding audience preferences and adapting content accordingly is a key element of successful content creation in today's digital landscape.

7.3 SEO Optimization for Content

Search Engine Optimization (SEO) is an integral part of content creation, ensuring that your content is discoverable and ranks well in search engine results. Google Bard provides content creators with valuable tools and techniques to optimize their content for SEO, helping them reach a broader audience.

1. Keyword Research

Keyword research is the foundation of SEO. Google Bard offers robust keyword research tools that help content creators identify relevant keywords and phrases that their target audience is searching for. These keywords can be strategically incorporated into content.

```
# Conducting keyword research for SEO
conductKeywordResearch()
identifyHigh-Volume Keywords()
```

2. On-Page SEO

Optimizing on-page elements is crucial. Google Bard provides guidance on optimizing title tags, meta descriptions, headers, and content structure to improve search engine rankings.

```
# On-page SEO optimization techniques
optimizeTitleTags()
craftCompellingMetaDescriptions()
structureContentEffectively()
```

3. Content Quality and Relevance

High-quality and relevant content is favored by search engines. Google Bard emphasizes the importance of creating valuable and informative content that addresses the needs and interests of your audience.

```
# Creating high-quality and relevant content
produceValuableContent()
addressAudienceNeeds()
```

4. Backlink Building

Backlinks from reputable sources enhance SEO. Google Bard offers strategies for building backlinks through guest posting, outreach, and content partnerships.

```
# Building backlinks for SEO improvement
executeGuestPosting()
conductOutreachCampaigns()
```

5. Mobile Optimization

Mobile-friendliness is a key SEO factor. Google Bard provides guidelines for ensuring that your content is accessible and well-optimized for mobile devices.

```
# Mobile optimization for improved SEO
optimizeForMobile()
testMobileResponsiveness()
```

6. Page Speed Optimization

Page loading speed is critical for SEO rankings. Google Bard offers insights and tools to improve page speed, such as image optimization and code minification.

```
# Optimizing page speed for SEO benefits
optimizeImages()
minifyCode()
```

7. SEO Plugins and Tools

Google Bard highlights the importance of using SEO plugins and tools that can assist content creators in optimizing their content for search engines, such as Yoast SEO and Google Search Console.

```
# Utilizing SEO plugins and tools
implementSEOTools()
analyzePerformanceMetrics()
```

8. Schema Markup

Implementing schema markup can enhance search engine visibility by providing structured data to search engines. Google Bard provides guidance on adding schema markup to content.

```
# Implementing schema markup for better search engine visibility
addStructuredData()
validateSchemaImplementation()
```

9. SEO Analytics

Measuring the impact of SEO efforts is essential. Google Bard offers analytics tools to track SEO performance, monitor keyword rankings, and assess traffic growth.

```
# Analyzing SEO performance through analytics
monitorKeywordRankings()
evaluateTrafficGrowth()
```

10. SEO Best Practices

Google Bard emphasizes the importance of staying updated with SEO best practices, algorithm changes, and industry trends to maintain and improve SEO rankings.

```
# Following SEO best practices and staying informed
stayUpdatedWithSEO()
adaptToAlgorithmChanges()
```

In conclusion, Google Bard equips content creators with valuable resources and techniques to optimize their content for SEO. By following these guidelines and utilizing SEO tools, content creators can enhance their content's discoverability, reach a broader audience, and improve their rankings on search engine results pages (SERPs). SEO optimization is a fundamental aspect of successful online content creation and is essential for achieving long-term visibility and growth in the digital landscape.

7.4 Monitoring Content Performance

Monitoring the performance of your content is a critical aspect of content creation and digital marketing. Google Bard offers content creators a range of tools and strategies to effectively track and evaluate the performance of their content. By regularly assessing how content is performing, creators can make data-driven decisions to improve engagement and reach their goals.

1. Website Analytics

Google Bard integrates with popular website analytics tools like Google Analytics, allowing content creators to track user behavior, page views, bounce rates, and other essential metrics. These insights provide a comprehensive view of how content is performing on your website.

```
# Integrating Google Analytics for website performance
tracking
integrateGoogleAnalytics()
analyzeUserBehavior()
```

2. Social Media Insights

For content shared on social media platforms, Google Bard provides access to social media insights. Creators can monitor likes, shares, comments, and other engagement metrics to gauge the impact of their social media content.

```
# Tracking social media insights for content performance
accessSocialMediaAnalytics()
measureSocialEngagement()
```

3. Email Campaign Analytics

For email marketing campaigns, Google Bard offers tools to track email open rates, click-through rates, and conversion rates. Monitoring email campaign performance is essential for optimizing email content.

```
# Monitoring email campaign performance through analytics
trackEmailOpenRates()
analyzeClick-ThroughRates()
```

4. Content A/B Testing

A/B testing is a powerful method for comparing the performance of two different content versions. Google Bard provides guidance on setting up A/B tests to determine which content variant performs better.

```
# Conducting A/B tests to optimize content performance
designContentExperiments()
evaluateTestResults()
```

5. Conversion Tracking

For content aimed at conversions (e.g., sign-ups, purchases), conversion tracking is crucial. Google Bard helps content creators set up conversion tracking to measure the effectiveness of call-to-action elements.

```
# Setting up conversion tracking for content with specific goals
configureConversionTracking()
analyzeConversionMetrics()
```

6. Heatmaps and User Behavior Analysis

Understanding how users interact with your content is essential. Google Bard offers tools to generate heatmaps and analyze user behavior, helping creators identify areas for improvement.

 # Analyzing user behavior through heatmaps and interaction data
```
generateHeatmaps()
assessUserInteractions()
```

7. SEO Performance Metrics

For content aimed at organic search traffic, SEO performance metrics are critical. Google Bard provides insights into keyword rankings, organic traffic growth, and click-through rates from search engine results pages (SERPs).

 # Monitoring SEO performance metrics for content visibility
```
trackKeywordRankings()
evaluateOrganicTrafficGrowth()
```

8. Content Engagement Metrics

Measuring content engagement is essential for assessing its impact. Google Bard offers tools to track metrics like views, likes, shares, and comments, providing insights into audience engagement.

 # Tracking content engagement metrics for audience interaction
```
monitorContentViews()
analyzeLikesAndShares()
evaluateCommentFeedback()
```

9. Performance Reports

Google Bard allows content creators to generate performance reports that consolidate data from various sources. These reports provide a holistic view of content performance and help in decision-making.

```
# Generating performance reports for comprehensive insi
ghts
createPerformanceReports()
analyzeReportData()
```

10. Continuous Improvement

Monitoring content performance should be an ongoing process. Google Bard emphasizes the importance of regularly reviewing performance data and making data-driven adjustments to content strategies.

```
# Continuously improving content based on performance d
ata
reviewPerformanceMetricsRegularly()
implementData-DrivenAdjustments()
```

In conclusion, Google Bard equips content creators with a suite of tools and strategies to monitor and evaluate content performance comprehensively. By harnessing these resources, content creators can gain valuable insights into how their content is resonating with their audience and make informed decisions to optimize their content for better results. Effective content performance monitoring is essential for achieving content marketing goals and ensuring continuous growth and engagement.

7.5 Collaborating and Sharing Insights

Collaboration is a key element in content creation and marketing. Google Bard offers various features and strategies for content creators to collaborate effectively with team members, share insights, and enhance their overall content creation process.

1. Shared Document and Workspace

Google Bard provides the capability to create shared documents and workspaces where team members can collaborate in real-time. These collaborative spaces allow for concurrent editing, commenting, and sharing of insights.

```
# Creating a shared document or workspace for collabora
tive content creation
createSharedDocument()
inviteTeamMembers()
collaborateInRealTime()
```

2. Comment and Feedback System

Within Google Bard's collaborative environment, content creators can leave comments and feedback on specific sections of content. This feature streamlines communication and ensures that feedback is targeted and actionable.

```
# Using the comment and feedback system for effective c
ollaboration
leaveCommentsAndFeedback()
addressFeedbackConcisely()
```

3. Version Control

Version control is crucial for managing changes and revisions in collaborative content projects. Google Bard offers version control tools to track and revert to previous versions of content when needed.

```
# Implementing version control for content revisions
trackContentVersions()
manageRevisionsEffectively()
```

4. Task Assignment and Management

Assigning tasks and responsibilities to team members is simplified with Google Bard's task assignment and management tools. Content creators can track progress and ensure that everyone is on the same page.

```
# Assigning tasks and tracking progress within the team
assignTasksToTeamMembers()
monitorTaskCompletion()
```

5. Integration with Project Management Tools

Google Bard seamlessly integrates with popular project management tools like Asana, Trello, or Jira. This integration allows content creators to manage content-related tasks within their preferred project management environment.

```
# Integrating Google Bard with project management tools for enhanced collaboration
connectToProjectManagementTools()
synchronizeTasksAndDeadlines()
```

6. Reporting and Insights Sharing

Sharing insights and performance reports is essential for informed decision-making. Google Bard enables content creators to generate and share performance reports with team members or stakeholders.

```
# Generating performance reports and sharing insights with stakeholders
createPerformanceReports()
distributeReportsToTeam()
discussInsightsCollaboratively()
```

7. Content Calendar Collaboration

Collaborating on a content calendar ensures that content creation is organized and aligned with marketing goals. Google Bard offers collaborative content calendar features to plan and schedule content effectively.

```
# Collaborating on a content calendar for organized content scheduling
createSharedContentCalendar()
scheduleContentCollaboratively()
```

8. Meeting Integration

For remote teams, Google Bard supports integration with virtual meeting platforms like Zoom or Microsoft Teams. This allows for real-time discussions and brainstorming sessions.

```
# Integrating virtual meetings for real-time collaborat
ion
connectToVirtualMeetingPlatforms()
conductMeetingsForIdeation()
```

9. Knowledge Sharing

Google Bard encourages knowledge sharing among team members. Content creators can document best practices, lessons learned, and valuable insights within the platform for reference and continuous improvement.

```
# Documenting knowledge and best practices for future r
eference
createKnowledgeBase()
shareValuableInsights()
```

10. Security and Access Control

While collaboration is essential, ensuring data security and access control is equally crucial. Google Bard provides robust security features to protect sensitive information and control who can access and edit content.

```
# Implementing security measures and access control
setAccessPermissions()
protectSensitiveData()
```

In summary, Google Bard offers a comprehensive set of features and strategies to facilitate collaboration and sharing of insights among content creators. Effective collaboration enhances content quality, streamlines workflows, and leads to more successful content marketing campaigns. Content creators can leverage these collaborative tools to work efficiently with their teams and create impactful content that resonates with their audience.

8.1 Addressing Search Accuracy Problems

Search accuracy is paramount when using Google Bard or any search engine. Ensuring that you receive relevant results that match your queries is essential for efficient information retrieval. In this section, we will explore common challenges related to search accuracy and strategies to address them effectively.

1. Query Refinement

One of the primary reasons for inaccurate search results is imprecise queries. Users may not always formulate their queries optimally, leading to irrelevant results. To address this, encourage users to refine their queries using techniques such as adding specific keywords, using quotation marks for exact phrases, or utilizing Boolean operators.

```
# Example of query refinement techniques
originalQuery = "best smartphones"
refinedQuery1 = "latest Android smartphones 2024"
refinedQuery2 = "\"iPhone 13 Pro Max\" reviews"
refinedQuery3 = "best smartphones AND budget under $500"
```

2. Filtering and Sorting

Google Bard provides various filtering and sorting options to help users narrow down search results. Encourage users to utilize these features to refine their results based on criteria like publication date, relevance, or location. Filters and sorting options can significantly improve the accuracy of information retrieval.

```
# Applying filters and sorting options to improve search accuracy
applyDateFilter()
```

```
sortResultsByRelevance()
filterByLocation()
```

3. Semantic Search

Semantic search is a powerful feature of Google Bard, allowing it to understand the context and intent behind a query. Users should be educated on how to frame their queries in a more natural language, enabling Google Bard to provide more accurate results.

```
# Example of semantic search query
userQuery = "Tell me about Van Gogh's famous sunflower paintings"
```

4. Utilizing Advanced Search Operators

Google Bard supports advanced search operators that can enhance search accuracy. These operators include "site:", "intitle:", and "filetype:". Users who are proficient in using these operators can achieve highly specific search results.

```
# Example of advanced search operators
userQuery = "site:wikipedia.org Albert Einstein"
userQuery2 = "intitle:\"Machine Learning\" filetype:pdf"
```

5. Feedback Mechanism

Implementing a feedback mechanism allows users to report inaccurate search results. Google Bard can use this feedback to improve its algorithms over time, ultimately enhancing search accuracy for all users.

```
# Providing a feedback mechanism for users to report inaccurate results
reportInaccurateResults()
utilizeUserFeedbackToImprove()
```

6. Continuous Learning

Educate users about the importance of continuous learning when it comes to refining search queries. Search technology evolves, and staying updated on best practices can lead to more accurate and efficient searches.

```
# Promoting continuous learning for better search accuracy
encourageUsersToLearn()
provideResourcesForImprovement()
```

7. Accessibility and User Assistance

Ensure that Google Bard offers accessible features and user assistance for individuals with disabilities or those who may struggle with search accuracy. Accessibility features can include voice commands, screen readers, and user-friendly interfaces.

```
# Implementing accessibility features and user assistance
provideVoiceCommandSupport()
integrateScreenReaders()
createUser-FriendlyInterfaces()
```

In conclusion, addressing search accuracy problems is vital for maximizing the utility of Google Bard. By educating users on query refinement, promoting the use of filters and sorting options, leveraging semantic search, utilizing advanced search operators, providing a feedback mechanism, promoting continuous learning, and ensuring accessibility, Google Bard can deliver more accurate and valuable search results to its users.

8.2 Handling Misunderstandings and Errors

Handling misunderstandings and errors in search results is crucial for providing a seamless user experience with Google Bard. Users may encounter situations where the search engine fails to understand their intent or provides inaccurate information. In this section, we will explore common issues related to misunderstandings and errors and strategies to effectively address them.

1. Query Clarification

Misunderstandings often arise from vague or ambiguous queries. Encourage users to clarify their queries with additional context or keywords. Google Bard's natural language processing capabilities can better understand and provide accurate results when queries are more explicit.

```
# Example of query clarification
ambiguousQuery = "apple"
clarifiedQuery = "apple Inc. stock price"
```

2. Error Messages and Suggestions

When Google Bard encounters a query it cannot understand or if there is a technical issue, it should provide clear error messages and suggestions for improvement. These messages can guide users on how to rephrase their queries or troubleshoot the issue.

```
# Providing clear error messages and suggestions
if (queryNotUnderstood):
    displayErrorMessage("We couldn't understand your query. Please try again with more details.")
    suggestQueryImprovements()
```

3. Search Query History

Allow users to access their search query history to review previous searches. This feature can help users identify and correct misunderstandings or errors in their queries. Additionally, it enables them to revisit past search results.

```
# Implementing search query history for users
displaySearchHistory()
revisitPreviousSearches()
```

4. User Feedback Loop

Establish a user feedback loop that enables users to report misunderstandings and errors. Google Bard can use this feedback to improve its understanding of user queries and provide more accurate results over time.

```
# Creating a user feedback loop for improving search accuracy
allowUserFeedback()
utilizeFeedbackToEnhanceUnderstanding()
```

5. Contextual Understanding

Enhance Google Bard's ability to understand context by considering previous queries and user behavior. By analyzing the user's search history and behavior, Google Bard can provide more relevant results, even when queries are vague.

```
# Utilizing contextual understanding for improved search results
analyzeUserBehavior()
considerPreviousQueries()
provideContextually RelevantResults()
```

6. User Assistance and Tutorials

Offer user assistance and tutorials that guide users on effective query formulation and troubleshooting. These resources can educate users on how to avoid common misunderstandings and errors.

```
# Providing user assistance and tutorials for query refinement
offerQueryFormulationGuidance()
educateUsersOnTroubleshooting()
```

7. Continuous Improvement

Emphasize the importance of continuous improvement in handling misunderstandings and errors. Google Bard should continually update its algorithms and models to better understand user queries and deliver more accurate results.

```
# Promoting continuous improvement for better user experience
focusOnAlgorithmEnhancements()
stayUpdatedWithNLPAdvancements()
```

In conclusion, addressing misunderstandings and errors in search results is essential for providing a satisfactory user experience with Google Bard. By encouraging query clarification, providing error messages and suggestions, implementing search query history, establishing a user feedback loop, enhancing contextual understanding, offering user assistance, and emphasizing continuous improvement, Google Bard can effectively handle misunderstandings and errors, ensuring users receive accurate and relevant information in their search results.

8.3 Updating User Preferences and Settings

User preferences and settings play a significant role in shaping the search experience with Google Bard. In this section, we will explore the importance of allowing users to customize their preferences and settings and provide guidance on how to implement and manage these options effectively.

1. Personalization

Allow users to personalize their Google Bard experience by adjusting settings such as language preferences, search history, and content filters. Personalization enhances user satisfaction by tailoring search results to individual preferences.

```
# Example of personalization settings
setLanguagePreference("English")
enableSearchHistory()
customizeContentFilters()
```

2. Privacy Settings

Offer robust privacy settings that allow users to control the amount of personal information they share with Google Bard. Ensure transparency in data collection practices and provide options for opting out of data collection if desired.

```
# Implementing privacy settings
controlDataCollectionPreferences()
informUsersAboutDataUsage()
provideOpt-OutOptions()
```

3. Notifications and Alerts

Enable users to configure notifications and alerts based on their interests and preferences. This feature ensures that users receive timely updates on topics they care about.

```
# Implementing notification and alert settings
setTopicPreferences()
configureAlertThresholds()
deliverCustomizedNotifications()
```

4. Accessibility Options

Ensure that Google Bard is accessible to users with diverse needs. Offer accessibility settings, such as screen reader compatibility and text-to-speech options, to accommodate users with disabilities.

```
# Providing accessibility options
enableScreenReaderCompatibility()
offerText-to-SpeechFunctionality()
supportKeyboardNavigation()
```

5. Search Results Display

Allow users to customize the way search results are displayed, including options for grid or list view, result snippet length, and thumbnail images. These settings enhance the user's ability to consume information efficiently.

```
# Customizing search results display
chooseGrid orListView()
adjustSnippetLength()
enableThumbnailPreviews()
```

6. Help and Support

Provide users with resources and assistance for managing their preferences and settings. Offer tutorials and guides on how to make the most of customization options and troubleshoot any issues that may arise.

```
# Offering help and support for managing preferences
createUserGuides()
offerCustomerSupportChannels()
resolveUserQueriesAboutSettings()
```

7. Consistent User Profile

Maintain a consistent user profile across devices and platforms by synchronizing user preferences and settings. This ensures that users' customization choices are seamlessly integrated into their Google Bard experience.

```
# Synchronizing user preferences across devices
maintainConsistentUserProfile()
enableCross-DeviceSync()
```

8. Default Settings

Choose default settings that align with the majority of users' preferences while respecting privacy and accessibility standards. Default settings should provide a good starting point for users who may not wish to customize their experience.

```
# Setting user-friendly default preferences
establishDefaultSettings()
balancePersonalization and Privacy
```

9. User Education

Educate users about the importance of customizing preferences and settings to enhance their search experience. Provide clear instructions on how to access and modify these options.

```
# Promoting user education on customization
highlightBenefitsOfCustomization()
offerIn-AppGuidance()
encourageExplorationOfSettings()
```

In conclusion, updating user preferences and settings is essential for creating a user-centric search experience with Google Bard. By offering personalization options, robust privacy settings, notifications and alerts, accessibility features, search results display customization, help and support resources, consistent user profiles, thoughtfully chosen default settings, and user education, Google Bard can empower users to tailor their search experience to their liking, ultimately leading to higher satisfaction and engagement.

8.4 Reporting Bugs and Providing Feedback

Reporting bugs and providing feedback is a crucial aspect of maintaining and improving Google Bard's search experience. In this section, we will discuss the significance of user feedback, how to encourage users to report bugs, and the best practices for handling and acting on feedback.

1. Importance of User Feedback

User feedback is a valuable source of information that helps identify issues, improve functionality, and enhance the overall user experience. Feedback can reveal problems that may not be immediately apparent to developers and designers, ensuring that Google Bard remains user-centric.

2. User-Friendly Feedback Mechanisms

Make it easy for users to report bugs and provide feedback within the Google Bard interface. Implement user-friendly feedback mechanisms, such as a dedicated "Report a Bug" button or a "Provide Feedback" option in the menu.

3. Clear Reporting Process

Outline a clear and straightforward process for users to follow when reporting bugs or providing feedback. Ensure that users understand the steps they need to take and the information they should include in their reports.

4. Bug Reporting Form

Create a bug reporting form that collects essential information from users, including the type of issue, a brief description, and steps to reproduce the problem. Include optional fields for users to attach screenshots or logs if applicable.

5. Anonymous Reporting Option

Offer users the option to provide feedback or report bugs anonymously. Some users may feel more comfortable sharing their experiences without revealing their identity.

6. Response Time

Set reasonable expectations for response times when users report bugs or provide feedback. Acknowledge receipt of the report promptly and provide a timeline for resolution or follow-up.

7. Categorization and Prioritization

Categorize incoming bug reports and feedback to prioritize them effectively. Identify critical issues that require immediate attention and non-critical ones that can be addressed in future updates.

8. Regular Bug Fix Releases

Frequently release bug fixes and updates to address reported issues. Keep users informed about bug fix releases and improvements through release notes or in-app notifications.

9. User Communication

Maintain open and transparent communication with users who have reported bugs or provided feedback. Update them on the status of their reports, inform them when issues are resolved, and express gratitude for their contributions.

10. Feedback Analysis

Analyze user feedback collectively to identify trends and recurring issues. Use this data to prioritize improvements and new features based on user needs and preferences.

11. Feedback Integration

Integrate user feedback into the development process. Ensure that feedback is considered when making decisions about feature enhancements and updates.

12. Feedback Loop

Establish a continuous feedback loop with users. Encourage them to provide ongoing feedback as they use Google Bard, and demonstrate that their input is valued and acted upon.

13. User Incentives

Consider offering incentives or rewards to users who actively participate in reporting bugs or providing valuable feedback. This can foster a sense of community and collaboration.

14. User Education

Educate users on the importance of reporting bugs and providing feedback for the improvement of Google Bard.

Highlight the positive impact their contributions can have on the product.

In conclusion, reporting bugs and providing feedback are integral to maintaining and enhancing Google Bard's search experience. By implementing user-friendly feedback mechanisms, establishing clear processes, responding promptly, categorizing and prioritizing issues, releasing regular bug fixes, maintaining transparent communication, analyzing feedback data, integrating feedback into development, fostering a continuous feedback loop, offering incentives, and educating users about the significance of their contributions, Google Bard can ensure that it continues to meet user needs and evolve to provide a seamless and reliable search experience.

8.5 Staying Informed About Updates and Changes

Staying informed about updates and changes in Google Bard is essential for users to make the most out of the search engine's evolving capabilities. In this section, we'll explore strategies to ensure that users are up-to-date with the latest features, improvements, and adjustments.

1. Release Notes

One of the primary sources of information about updates and changes is the release notes. Google Bard should provide detailed release notes with each update, highlighting what's new, improved, and fixed. These notes can be accessed within the application or on the official website.

2. In-App Notifications

Implement in-app notifications to alert users about significant updates or changes. These notifications should provide a brief summary of the update and a link to the full release notes for those interested in more details.

3. Email Updates

Allow users to subscribe to email updates from Google Bard. This way, they can receive news about updates, new features, and important changes directly in their inbox. Ensure that users can easily opt-in or opt-out of these emails.

4. Blog or News Section

Maintain a blog or news section on the Google Bard website. Regularly publish articles or posts about updates, changes, and feature highlights. Include practical tips on how to make the most of new features.

5. Social Media Channels

Leverage social media platforms to share updates and engage with the Google Bard user community. Create official profiles on popular social networks and regularly post about product news, events, and user success stories.

6. Webinars and Tutorials

Host webinars or create video tutorials to showcase new features and changes. Provide step-by-step guides on how to use them effectively. Record these sessions for users who cannot attend live.

7. User Community Forums

Encourage users to participate in Google Bard's community forums. These forums can serve as a hub for users to discuss updates, share tips, and ask questions. Official representatives should actively engage with the community to address queries.

8. Feedback and Suggestions

Incorporate a feedback mechanism within Google Bard that allows users to provide suggestions for improvements. This feedback can help prioritize future updates and changes based on user needs and preferences.

9. Regular Newsletters

Send out regular newsletters to subscribers, summarizing recent updates and changes. Include links to relevant resources, such as blog posts, tutorials, and release notes, for users who want more information.

10. Customer Support

Ensure that the customer support team is well-informed about updates and changes. They should be able to assist users with questions or issues related to the new features. Prompt and helpful support enhances the user experience.

11. Transparency

Maintain transparency about the reasons behind specific changes or adjustments. When users understand the rationale, they are more likely to adapt to and appreciate the updates.

12. User Surveys

Periodically conduct user surveys to gather feedback on recent changes and gauge user satisfaction. Use the insights gained to refine future updates and prioritize improvements.

13. Update Frequency

Determine a predictable update frequency to set user expectations. Whether updates are monthly, quarterly, or at another interval, consistency is key to keeping users informed.

14. Beta Testing Programs

Consider launching beta testing programs for select users who want to experience and provide feedback on new features before they are widely released. This can help iron out any issues before the full rollout.

15. Accessibility

Ensure that all information about updates and changes is easily accessible within the Google Bard interface. Users should not have to search extensively to find this information.

In conclusion, staying informed about updates and changes in Google Bard is vital for users to maximize their search experience. By providing comprehensive release notes, in-app notifications, email updates, blog posts, social media engagement, webinars, user community forums, feedback mechanisms, newsletters, customer support, transparency, user surveys, predictable update frequencies, beta testing programs, and accessible information, Google Bard can empower users to make the most of its evolving capabilities while maintaining a satisfied and engaged user base.

9.1 Understanding Data Collection and Use

Understanding how data is collected and used in Google Bard is crucial for users who are concerned about their privacy and want to make informed decisions about their online activities. In this section, we will delve into the key aspects of data collection and usage within Google Bard.

Data Collection Principles

Google Bard collects user data with the primary aim of improving the search experience and providing more personalized results. The following principles guide data collection:

1. **Relevance**: Data collected is directly related to improving search quality, relevance, and user experience.

2. **Anonymization**: Personal information is anonymized and aggregated to protect user privacy.

3. **Opt-in**: Users have the option to opt-in or opt-out of certain data collection features.

4. **Transparency**: Google Bard is transparent about the types of data collected and how it is used.

5. **Consent**: Data collection features that require user consent explicitly ask for permission.

Types of Data Collected

Google Bard collects several types of data, including:

1. Search Queries

When you use Google Bard, your search queries are recorded. This data helps improve search results and predict user intent.

2. Location Information

If location services are enabled, Google Bard may collect location data to provide more relevant local search results.

3. Usage Statistics

Data on how you interact with Google Bard, such as the features you use and the time spent on the platform, is collected for analytics.

4. Device Information

Information about the device you're using, including hardware and software details, may be collected for compatibility and optimization purposes.

5. Personalization Data

If you opt-in, Google Bard may collect data to personalize your search results and suggestions, such as your search history and preferences.

6. Cookies and Tracking

Cookies and similar tracking technologies may be used to improve user experience and gather analytics data.

Data Usage

The data collected in Google Bard serves various purposes:

1. Improving Search Quality

User data helps Google Bard understand search intent, leading to better search results.

2. Personalization

Data is used to personalize search results, suggestions, and ads based on user preferences.

3. Analytics

Usage data helps Google Bard analyze user behavior, identify trends, and optimize the platform.

4. Ad Targeting

For users who opt-in, data may be used to deliver more relevant advertisements.

Privacy Settings

Google Bard provides privacy settings to give users control over their data. These settings include:

- **Data Deletion**: Users can delete their search history and associated data.
- **Opt-Out**: Users can opt-out of personalized search results and ads.
- **Location Control**: Users can manage location settings to control when location data is shared.

Security Measures

Google Bard employs robust security measures to protect user data from unauthorized access and breaches. These measures include encryption, regular security audits, and compliance with privacy regulations.

User Responsibility

While Google Bard takes data privacy seriously, users also have a responsibility to protect their data. This includes using strong passwords, enabling two-factor authentication, and being cautious about sharing personal information online.

In conclusion, understanding data collection and usage in Google Bard is essential for informed use of the search engine. Google Bard adheres to principles of relevance, anonymization, opt-in, transparency, and consent when collecting data. Users should be aware of the types of data collected, the purposes it serves, and the available privacy settings to make informed choices about their online activities while using the platform.

Managing Your Digital Footprint

In an increasingly digital world, managing your digital footprint is a vital aspect of online privacy and security. Your digital footprint refers to the trail of data and information you leave behind when you interact with websites, apps, and online services. In this section, we'll explore the significance of managing your digital footprint and provide tips on how to do it effectively.

Why Manage Your Digital Footprint?

1. **Privacy Protection**: Managing your digital footprint helps safeguard your personal information from unauthorized access and data breaches.

2. **Identity Theft Prevention**: Minimizing your online presence reduces the risk of identity theft, where malicious actors use your information for fraudulent purposes.

3. **Reduced Targeted Advertising**: A smaller digital footprint means you're less likely to receive invasive targeted ads based on your online activities.

4. **Enhanced Online Security**: Limiting the amount of personal information available online reduces the chances of cyberattacks and phishing attempts.

Tips for Managing Your Digital Footprint

1. Review Privacy Settings

Regularly review and adjust the privacy settings on your social media profiles, email accounts, and other online platforms. Limit the amount of personal information visible to the public.

2. Use Strong, Unique Passwords

Employ strong and unique passwords for your online accounts to prevent unauthorized access. Consider using a reputable password manager to help you generate and store complex passwords.

3. Enable Two-Factor Authentication (2FA)

Whenever possible, enable 2FA on your online accounts. This additional layer of security ensures that even if your password is compromised, access to your accounts remains protected.

4. Limit Sharing Personal Information

Be cautious about sharing personal information, such as your full name, address, phone number, and financial details, on websites and social media platforms. Only share such information with trusted sources.

5. Regularly Delete or Update Old Accounts

Review the online accounts you no longer use and either delete them or update the information to minimize your digital footprint.

6. Use Anonymous Browsing

When browsing the web, consider using private or incognito browsing modes to prevent websites from tracking your activity and storing cookies.

7. Educate Yourself

Stay informed about online privacy practices and data protection laws in your region. Knowledge is a powerful tool in safeguarding your digital footprint.

8. Monitor Your Online Presence

Regularly search for your name and personal information online to see what information is publicly available. Take steps to remove or update inaccurate or outdated information.

9. Be Cautious with Social Media

Exercise caution when sharing personal information, photos, and updates on social media. Review your friends and followers to ensure you're only connecting with trusted individuals.

10. Use Encrypted Messaging Apps
Consider using encrypted messaging apps for private conversations to protect your communication from eavesdropping.

Conclusion

Managing your digital footprint is an ongoing process that requires vigilance and awareness of your online activities. By implementing these tips and being mindful of what you share and where you share it, you can take control of your online presence and protect your privacy in the digital age.

Security Features and Protocols

Ensuring the security of your online activities and data is paramount in today's digital landscape. Section 9.3 delves into various security features and protocols that can help you protect your personal information and maintain online security.

1. Encryption

Encryption is a fundamental security feature that protects your data by converting it into an unreadable format that can only be deciphered with the correct encryption key. It plays a crucial role in securing communications, such as emails and messages, and safeguarding sensitive information during transmission.

Example: Encrypting Email Communication

You can use email services that support end-to-end encryption, such as PGP (Pretty Good Privacy) or S/MIME (Secure/Multipurpose Internet Mail Extensions), to encrypt your email messages. This ensures that only the intended recipient can read the message.

2. Virtual Private Networks (VPNs)

VPNs create a secure and private network connection over the internet. They are effective tools for protecting your online activities from prying eyes, especially when using public Wi-Fi networks.

Example: Using a VPN for Privacy

When connecting to a public Wi-Fi network, activate your VPN to encrypt your internet traffic and keep your data secure from potential eavesdroppers.

3. Two-Factor Authentication (2FA)

2FA adds an extra layer of security by requiring you to provide two different authentication factors (usually something you know, like a password, and something you have, like a mobile device) before granting access to your accounts.

Example: Activating 2FA for Online Accounts

Enable 2FA on your email, social media, and financial accounts to prevent unauthorized access, even if someone has your password.

4. Strong Password Practices

Creating strong and unique passwords for your online accounts is essential. Passwords should be lengthy and include a combination of uppercase and lowercase letters, numbers, and special characters.

Example: Using a Password Manager

Consider using a reputable password manager to generate, store, and autofill complex passwords for your various accounts.

5. Security Updates and Patching

Regularly update your operating system, software, and applications to patch security vulnerabilities. Cybercriminals often target outdated software with known vulnerabilities.

Example: Keeping Software Up to Date

Set your devices and applications to automatically receive updates to ensure you have the latest security patches.

6. Firewalls

Firewalls act as barriers between your device and potentially harmful internet traffic. They can be implemented at the hardware or software level.

Example: Configuring a Firewall

Configure your device's built-in firewall or install a reputable third-party firewall to monitor and filter incoming and outgoing network traffic.

7. Secure Browsing Practices

Practice safe browsing by being cautious about the websites you visit, avoiding suspicious links and downloads, and using browser security features like pop-up blockers and phishing protection.

Example: Verifying Website URLs

Before entering personal information or login credentials, verify that the website's URL starts with "https://" to ensure a secure connection.

8. Data Backups

Regularly back up your important data to an external storage device or cloud service. In the event of data loss due to cyberattacks or hardware failures, backups can be a lifesaver.

Example: Automating Backups

Use automated backup solutions to ensure that your data is consistently and securely backed up without manual intervention.

9. Online Shopping and Financial Transactions

When making online purchases or conducting financial transactions, use reputable websites and payment methods that offer enhanced security features.

Example: Using Secure Payment Services

Prefer using payment methods like PayPal or secure credit card processors that provide buyer protection and encryption for online transactions.

10. Security Awareness and Education

Stay informed about the latest cybersecurity threats and best practices through online resources, courses, and community forums.

Example: Taking Online Security Courses

Enroll in online courses or attend webinars on cybersecurity to enhance your knowledge and protect yourself effectively.

Conclusion

By incorporating these security features and protocols into your online activities, you can significantly enhance your digital security and reduce the risks associated with cyber threats. Remember that online security is an ongoing commitment, and staying vigilant is key to protecting your personal information in an increasingly interconnected world.

Best Practices for Protecting Personal Information

Protecting your personal information is crucial in today's digital age, where data breaches and privacy concerns are widespread. This section, Section 9.4, discusses best practices for safeguarding your personal information online.

1. Data Minimization

One effective way to protect your personal information is to practice data minimization. Only share the information that is absolutely necessary when signing up for online services or making transactions. Avoid providing excessive personal details.

Example: Online Forms

When filling out online forms, provide the minimum required information. If optional fields exist, consider leaving them blank.

2. Privacy Settings

Familiarize yourself with the privacy settings of the online platforms and services you use. Adjust these settings to control who can access your information and how it is shared.

Example: Social Media Privacy

Review and customize the privacy settings on your social media profiles to limit the visibility of your posts and personal information to a select audience.

3. Secure Wi-Fi Networks

Be cautious when connecting to Wi-Fi networks, especially public ones. Use secure, password-protected networks whenever possible, and avoid connecting to open, unsecured networks.

Example: Mobile Hotspots

If you must use public Wi-Fi, consider using a mobile hotspot with password protection to create a secure connection for your devices.

4. Phishing Awareness

Be vigilant against phishing attempts. Phishing emails and websites often mimic legitimate sources to trick you into revealing sensitive information.

Example: Email Verification

Verify the sender's email address and check for spelling errors or unusual requests in emails before clicking on any links or providing information.

5. Password Hygiene

Practice good password hygiene by using strong, unique passwords for each of your online accounts. Avoid using easily guessable information like birthdays or names.

Example: Password Managers

Consider using a reputable password manager to generate and securely store complex passwords for your various accounts.

6. Multi-Factor Authentication (MFA)

Enable multi-factor authentication (MFA) whenever possible. MFA adds an extra layer of security by requiring you to provide multiple forms of authentication.

Example: Authentication Apps

Use authentication apps like Google Authenticator or Authy to generate time-based codes for MFA.

7. Regularly Monitor Accounts

Regularly monitor your bank accounts, credit card statements, and online accounts for any unauthorized or suspicious activity. Report any discrepancies immediately.

Example: Account Alerts

Set up account alerts for unusual activity, such as large transactions or login attempts from unfamiliar locations.

8. App Permissions

Review and manage the permissions granted to mobile apps on your devices. Some apps may request unnecessary access to your personal information.

Example: App Permissions

When installing or updating apps, review the permissions they request and consider whether they are justified.

9. Secure File Storage

If you store sensitive documents or files digitally, ensure they are encrypted and stored securely. Use reputable cloud storage providers with strong encryption measures.

Example: Encrypted Cloud Storage

Choose cloud storage services that offer end-to-end encryption to protect your files from unauthorized access.

10. Keep Software Updated

Regularly update your operating system, software, and antivirus programs. These updates often include security patches that protect against known vulnerabilities.

Example: Automatic Updates

Enable automatic updates on your devices and applications to ensure you receive the latest security fixes.

Conclusion

Implementing these best practices can significantly enhance your ability to protect your personal information and reduce the risk of falling victim to cyber threats and privacy breaches. Stay informed about evolving security measures and remain vigilant to maintain control over your online privacy and security.

The Future of Privacy in AI-Powered Search

As we move further into the digital age, the intersection of privacy and AI-powered search becomes increasingly critical. Section 9.5 explores the future of privacy in AI-powered search and the potential developments and challenges that lie ahead.

1. Enhanced Privacy Controls

The future of AI-powered search will likely see the development of more advanced privacy controls. Users will have greater flexibility in defining how their data is used and shared, with options to customize data retention periods and control who can access their search history.

Example: Granular Privacy Settings

Users may be able to specify which types of data can be used for personalized recommendations and which should be kept entirely private.

2. Differential Privacy

Differential privacy is an emerging concept that aims to protect user data while still enabling valuable insights for AI models. In the future, AI-powered search engines may implement differential privacy techniques to anonymize user data effectively.

Example: Privacy-Preserving Analytics

Search engines can provide aggregated analytics to advertisers without revealing individual user behaviors.

3. Federated Learning

Federated learning allows AI models to be trained across decentralized devices without centralizing user data. This approach may become more prevalent in AI-powered search to enhance privacy.

Example: Local Model Updates

User devices can perform model updates locally, sharing only model improvements rather than raw data with the central server.

4. Blockchain for Data Control

Blockchain technology may play a role in giving users greater control over their search data. Users could have a blockchain-based identity and granular control over who accesses their data.

Example: Consent Smart Contracts

Users can create smart contracts that specify under what conditions their data can be used and for what purposes.

5. Ethical AI and Transparency

Future AI-powered search engines will need to prioritize ethical AI practices and transparency. Users should have a clear understanding of how their data is used and how search results are generated.

Example: Transparency Reports

Search engines may provide transparency reports detailing data usage, algorithm changes, and adherence to ethical guidelines.

6. Legislation and Regulation

As concerns about privacy grow, governments and regulatory bodies may enact stricter legislation to protect user data. Companies providing AI-powered search services will need to comply with these regulations.

Example: GDPR-Like Regulations

New privacy regulations may require explicit user consent for data collection and impose hefty fines for non-compliance.

7. Privacy-Centric Search Engines

The future may witness the emergence of privacy-centric search engines that prioritize user privacy above all else. These search engines could gain popularity among users seeking maximum data protection.

Example: Subscription-Based Models

Privacy-focused search engines may adopt subscription-based models to reduce reliance on ad-based data collection.

8. User Education

Education will continue to be a crucial aspect of the future of privacy in AI-powered search. Users need to be informed about the risks and benefits of sharing their data and how to protect themselves online.

Example: Privacy Literacy Programs

Schools and organizations may offer privacy literacy programs to educate users about online privacy best practices.

9. Privacy-Enhancing Technologies

Technologies specifically designed to enhance privacy, such as secure hardware and encryption, will become more integrated into AI-powered search infrastructure.

Example: End-to-End Encryption

End-to-end encryption may become standard for search queries and results to prevent data interception.

10. Collaborative Efforts

Companies, researchers, and governments will need to collaborate to address privacy challenges collectively. An open dialogue and cooperation are essential for shaping a more privacy-conscious AI-powered search ecosystem.

Example: Privacy Research Consortia

Consortia and research initiatives may form to explore and develop privacy-preserving technologies for AI in search.

Conclusion

The future of privacy in AI-powered search holds promise for enhanced user control and protection. However, it also presents challenges that require continuous innovation, collaboration, and ethical considerations. As AI-powered search continues to evolve, prioritizing user privacy will be paramount to building trust and ensuring a responsible and secure digital future.

Incorporating Bard into Classroom Learning

In this section, we delve into the integration of Google Bard into classroom learning environments. Educators, students, and institutions are increasingly recognizing the potential of AI-powered search engines like Bard to enhance the learning experience. This section explores the various ways in which Bard can be incorporated into the classroom to facilitate teaching and learning.

1. Personalized Learning

One of the primary benefits of using Bard in the classroom is its ability to provide personalized learning experiences. Educators can encourage students to use Bard for research, allowing them to explore topics of interest at their own pace. Bard's ability to understand natural language queries makes it easy for students to find relevant information quickly.

Example: Research Projects

Students can use Bard to find scholarly articles, books, and online resources related to their research projects, saving time and effort in information gathering.

2. Facilitating Discussion

Bard can serve as a valuable tool for initiating and facilitating classroom discussions. Educators can use Bard to find up-to-date articles, news, or research papers related to the topics being discussed in class. This provides students with fresh insights and encourages critical thinking.

Example: Current Events

In a history class, an educator can use Bard to find recent news articles about historical events, sparking discussions about their relevance and impact on the present.

3. Supporting Homework and Assignments

Assignments and homework often require students to gather information and conduct research. Bard can streamline this process by providing students with relevant sources and references. Educators can recommend specific search queries to guide students effectively.

Example: Essay Writing

When students are tasked with writing essays, Bard can help them find academic sources, statistics, and quotes to strengthen their arguments.

4. Encouraging Digital Literacy

Incorporating Bard into classroom learning also contributes to students' digital literacy. Educators can teach students how to formulate effective search queries, evaluate the credibility of sources, and critically analyze search results.

Example: Search Strategy Workshops

Educators can organize workshops on search strategies, helping students develop skills that are valuable not only in academia but also in their future careers.

5. Preparing for Research Projects

For more extended research projects or theses, Bard can be an invaluable asset. Educators can guide students in using Bard's advanced search techniques, citation management, and note-taking features to organize their research effectively.

Example: Research Workshops

Educators can conduct workshops on using Bard's advanced features, ensuring that students are well-prepared for their research endeavors.

6. Collaborative Learning

Bard supports collaborative learning by enabling students to share search results and resources with their peers. This fosters teamwork and knowledge sharing within the classroom.

Example: Group Projects

Students working on group projects can use Bard to collectively gather and organize research materials, enhancing their collaboration and productivity.

7. Assessment and Evaluation

Educators can use Bard's search history and saved resources to assess students' research efforts. This provides insights into students' information retrieval skills and the quality of sources they utilize.

Example: Research Portfolios

Educators may ask students to maintain research portfolios, including their search histories, to showcase their information gathering process.

8. Accessibility and Inclusivity

Bard's natural language processing capabilities make it accessible to a wide range of students, including those with different learning styles and abilities. It can assist students in finding information in formats that suit their preferences.

Example: Audiobooks and Summaries

Students with visual impairments or reading difficulties can use Bard to find audiobooks or summaries of academic texts.

Conclusion

Incorporating Google Bard into classroom learning offers numerous advantages, from personalized learning experiences to enhanced digital literacy. Educators and institutions can harness the power of AI-powered search to empower students, improve research skills, and create more engaging and effective learning environments. As technology continues to play a significant role in education, integrating AI-powered search engines like Bard becomes increasingly important for educators and students alike.

Facilitating Research and Study

In this section, we will explore how Google Bard can be a valuable tool for facilitating research and study for students across various academic disciplines. Whether you're a high school student preparing for exams or a university researcher delving into complex topics, Bard can assist you in finding, organizing, and comprehending information effectively.

1. Comprehensive Information Retrieval

One of the primary advantages of using Bard for research and study is its ability to provide comprehensive and up-to-date information on a wide range of topics. You can use Bard to explore academic journals, books, websites, and other resources, ensuring that you have access to the latest research findings and scholarly materials.

2. Efficient Literature Reviews

When conducting literature reviews for research papers or projects, Bard can streamline the process. You can use specific search queries to identify key publications and studies relevant to your research topic, saving time and effort in sifting through extensive databases.

3. Organizing Research Materials

Bard's features for saving and organizing research materials are invaluable. You can create digital libraries of articles, papers, and references, making it easy to retrieve and cite sources when writing essays, reports, or dissertations.

4. Advanced Search Techniques

For more advanced research, Bard offers advanced search techniques. You can use operators like "AND," "OR," and "NOT" to refine your queries and narrow down search results. Additionally, you can use quotation marks to search for exact phrases, ensuring precision in your research.

Example: Advanced Query

Suppose you're researching the impact of climate change on coastal ecosystems. You can use Bard to construct a query like:

```
"climate change" AND "coastal ecosystems" NOT "urban development"
```

This query helps you find sources specifically related to climate change and coastal ecosystems while excluding irrelevant information about urban development.

5. Citation Management

Managing citations and references is an essential part of academic research. Bard offers tools to help you cite sources correctly, ensuring that your work adheres to academic standards. You can easily generate citations in various citation styles, such as APA, MLA, or Chicago.

6. Collaborative Research

For group projects or collaborative research efforts, Bard enables seamless sharing of research materials with team members. You can create shared folders or documents, allowing everyone in the group to access and contribute to the research process.

7. Staying Informed

Bard's notification and alert features keep you informed about new research publications and developments in your field of interest. You can set up alerts for specific keywords or topics, ensuring that you're always up to date with the latest research.

8. Enhancing Critical Thinking

Using Bard for research encourages critical thinking and analysis. As you explore various sources and viewpoints, you develop the ability to evaluate the credibility of information and synthesize knowledge from diverse perspectives.

Example: Evaluating Sources

When using Bard, it's essential to assess the credibility of sources. Look for publications from reputable journals or academic institutions, check author credentials, and consider the publication date to ensure the information is current.

9. Access to Diverse Formats

Bard provides access to information in diverse formats, including text, images, videos, and more. This versatility allows you to engage with content in a way that suits your learning style and preferences.

10. Preparing for Exams

Students can use Bard to prepare for exams by accessing study guides, practice tests, and educational resources related to their courses. Whether you're studying for a history exam or a mathematics test, Bard can assist you in finding relevant materials.

Conclusion

Google Bard serves as a powerful ally in the world of research and study. Its ability to retrieve comprehensive information, assist in literature reviews, organize research materials, and promote critical thinking makes it an indispensable tool for students and researchers alike. By harnessing the capabilities of Bard, individuals can enhance their academic pursuits and make informed contributions to their respective fields.

Encouraging Critical Thinking and Analysis

In this section, we will delve into the role of Google Bard in encouraging critical thinking and analysis among students and learners across different educational levels. Critical thinking is a vital skill that involves evaluating information, making reasoned judgments, and solving complex problems. Google Bard provides several features and tools that can facilitate the development of these essential skills.

1. Diverse Sources of Information

One of the fundamental ways Google Bard promotes critical thinking is by providing access to a wide range of information sources. When researching a topic or question, users can explore various viewpoints, opinions, and data, encouraging them to consider multiple perspectives before forming conclusions.

2. Evaluating Source Credibility

Critical thinking involves assessing the credibility and reliability of information sources. Google Bard users learn to distinguish between reputable sources, such as peer-reviewed journals and established institutions, and less reliable sources. This skill is invaluable in avoiding misinformation and biased information.

3. Analyzing and Synthesizing Information

Students and learners can use Bard to gather information from different sources and analyze it comprehensively. They learn to identify key insights, patterns, and trends by comparing and contrasting various pieces of information. This process of synthesis is crucial for making informed decisions and drawing meaningful conclusions.

4. Questioning and Inquiry

Google Bard encourages users to ask questions and engage in inquiry-based learning. Instead of passively consuming information, learners can initiate searches with specific questions in mind, leading to more focused and in-depth exploration of topics. This approach fosters curiosity and a thirst for knowledge.

Example: Inquiry-Based Learning

Suppose a high school student is studying climate change. Instead of searching for general information, the student can pose specific questions like, "What are the causes of sea-level rise due to climate change?" or "How do climate change impacts vary across different regions?" These questions drive focused research and critical analysis.

5. Fact-Checking and Debunking Misinformation

In an era of information overload, critical thinking involves fact-checking and debunking misinformation. Google Bard users can verify claims, cross-reference information, and identify false or misleading content, contributing to digital literacy and responsible information consumption.

6. Ethical Considerations

Critical thinking also encompasses ethical considerations when using and sharing information. Bard users are encouraged to think about the ethical implications of their research, including issues related to privacy, bias, and data use. This ethical awareness is essential in the responsible use of information.

7. Problem-Solving Skills

Google Bard can assist learners in developing problem-solving skills by providing access to solutions, best practices, and case studies. Whether solving math problems, addressing complex issues in science, or finding innovative solutions to real-world challenges, Bard offers valuable resources.

8. Encouraging Discussion and Debate

In educational settings, Bard can be used to stimulate discussion and debate. Teachers and instructors can assign research projects or topics, prompting students to explore different perspectives and present arguments based on their findings. This process fosters critical analysis and effective communication skills.

9. Lifelong Learning

The critical thinking skills acquired through Google Bard extend beyond formal education. Individuals can carry these skills into their professional lives, making informed decisions, solving complex problems, and adapting to evolving information landscapes.

Conclusion

Google Bard plays a significant role in nurturing critical thinking and analysis among students and learners. By providing access to diverse sources of information, encouraging source evaluation, promoting inquiry-based learning, and fostering ethical considerations, Bard empowers individuals to become informed, discerning, and analytical thinkers. These skills are not only valuable in academia but also in everyday life and professional endeavors, contributing to a more informed and responsible society.

Balancing Technology and Traditional Learning Methods

In this section, we'll explore the importance of striking a balance between technology, represented by Google Bard, and traditional learning methods within educational institutions. While Google Bard offers numerous advantages, it's essential to consider how it can complement, rather than replace, traditional teaching and learning approaches.

1. Enhancing Traditional Teaching

Google Bard can serve as a valuable tool to enhance traditional teaching methods. Educators can incorporate Bard into their lesson plans to provide supplementary resources, encourage research, and facilitate interactive discussions. This integration allows students to benefit from both structured classroom instruction and self-directed learning.

2. Supporting Personalized Learning

One of Bard's strengths is its ability to cater to individual learning styles and paces. Students can use Bard to explore topics at their own speed, revisiting content as needed. This personalized learning experience complements the one-size-fits-all approach of traditional classrooms, ensuring that each student's needs are addressed.

3. Fostering Collaborative Learning

While traditional learning often occurs in isolation, Bard promotes collaborative learning. Students can collaborate on research projects, share insights, and engage in discussions with peers and educators through digital platforms. This collaborative environment encourages knowledge sharing and the development of teamwork skills.

4. Bridging Gaps in Access to Information

In many educational settings, access to resources can be limited, especially in underprivileged areas. Google Bard's accessibility can help bridge these gaps by providing students with access to a wealth of information, regardless of their physical location. This democratization of knowledge is a significant advantage.

5. Preparing Students for the Digital Age

In today's world, digital literacy and proficiency are essential skills. Integrating Google Bard into the curriculum ensures that students are familiar with advanced search techniques, critical evaluation of online sources, and responsible use of digital resources. These skills are invaluable in the digital age.

6. Addressing Challenges and Concerns

While technology-enhanced learning offers numerous benefits, it's essential to address challenges and concerns. These may include issues related to privacy, digital distractions, overreliance on technology, and the need for guidance in navigating the vast sea of online information. Educational institutions should provide guidance and resources to address these challenges effectively.

7. Professional Development for Educators

Educators themselves can benefit from Google Bard's capabilities. They can undergo professional development programs to harness the full potential of Bard in teaching and research. Training programs can equip teachers and instructors with the skills needed to create engaging and effective digital learning experiences.

8. Encouraging a Growth Mindset

Balancing technology and traditional methods encourages a growth mindset among students and educators. It fosters adaptability and a willingness to embrace new tools and methods while valuing the foundations of traditional education.

This mindset is crucial in preparing individuals for a rapidly evolving educational landscape.

9. Measuring the Impact

To ensure the effectiveness of integrating Google Bard, educational institutions should regularly assess its impact on student learning outcomes. Surveys, performance evaluations, and feedback mechanisms can provide insights into whether Bard is contributing to improved critical thinking, research skills, and overall educational quality.

10. Continuous Improvement

The integration of Google Bard should be an ongoing process. Educational institutions should continuously evaluate and refine their approaches to maximize the benefits of technology while preserving the core values of traditional education. Flexibility and adaptability are key to success in this endeavor.

Conclusion

Balancing technology, represented by Google Bard, with traditional learning methods is a strategic approach that leverages the strengths of both worlds. It enhances teaching, supports personalized learning, fosters collaboration, addresses information gaps, and prepares students for the digital age. By recognizing the value of both traditional and digital education, educational institutions can create a holistic and effective learning environment that equips students with the skills and knowledge needed for success in the 21st century.

Preparing Students for an AI-Driven World

In this section, we will delve into the critical role of preparing students for an AI-driven world and how educators can use Google Bard as a tool to achieve this objective. The rise of artificial intelligence (AI) and machine learning is transforming various industries and reshaping the employment landscape. It is imperative that educational institutions equip students with the skills, knowledge, and mindset required to thrive in this evolving environment.

1. AI Literacy and Awareness

One of the primary responsibilities of educators is to foster AI literacy and awareness among students. This involves introducing students to the fundamental concepts of AI, its applications across domains, and its societal implications. Understanding the basics of AI is crucial for informed decision-making and career choices.

2. Integrating AI into the Curriculum

Educational institutions can integrate AI-related topics and projects into their curricula. This includes offering courses or modules that explore AI, machine learning, and natural language processing. Students should have opportunities to engage with AI technologies hands-on, allowing them to develop practical skills.

```python
# Example of a simple Python code for AI education
import tensorflow as tf
from tensorflow import keras

# Define a basic neural network model
model = keras.Sequential([
    keras.layers.Input(shape=(784,)),
    keras.layers.Dense(128, activation='relu'),
    keras.layers.Dense(10, activation='softmax')
])

# Compile the model
model.compile(optimizer='adam',
              loss='sparse_categorical_crossentropy',
              metrics=['accuracy'])
```

3. Problem-Solving and Critical Thinking

AI-driven solutions are often employed to tackle complex problems. Educators should emphasize problem-solving and critical thinking skills in the classroom. Students should learn how to identify challenges that can be addressed with AI and devise innovative solutions.

4. Ethical AI Use

Understanding the ethical considerations surrounding AI is paramount. Students should be aware of issues related to bias, fairness, transparency, and privacy in AI systems. Educational institutions can foster discussions and projects that explore the ethical dimensions of AI technology.

5. Collaboration and Interdisciplinary Learning

AI projects often require collaboration among individuals with diverse skills. Encouraging interdisciplinary learning can prepare students for careers that involve working with AI. For example, computer science students can collaborate with social scientists or healthcare professionals to develop AI-driven healthcare solutions.

6. Lifelong Learning Mindset

Given the rapid advancements in AI, it is crucial to instill a lifelong learning mindset in students. They should understand that their education does not end with graduation but continues throughout their careers. AI professionals must continuously update their knowledge and skills to stay relevant.

7. Real-World Applications

Connecting classroom learning to real-world applications of AI is essential. Students can benefit from internships, projects, or industry collaborations that expose them to AI in practice. This hands-on experience helps bridge the gap between theory and application.

```python
# Real-world AI application example: Autonomous vehicle
control
class AutonomousVehicle:
    def __init__(self):
        self.speed = 0
        self.direction = 'forward'

    def accelerate(self):
        self.speed += 1

    def decelerate(self):
        self.speed -= 1

    def change_direction(self, new_direction):
        self.direction = new_direction

    def navigate(self):
        # AI-driven navigation logic goes here
        pass
```

8. Soft Skills and Adaptability

In addition to technical skills, soft skills such as adaptability, communication, and teamwork are vital. AI professionals often work in dynamic environments and must effectively communicate their findings and solutions to non-technical stakeholders.

9. Encouraging Innovation

Educational institutions should create an environment that encourages innovation. Students should feel empowered to explore new ideas and experiment with AI technologies. This fosters creativity and entrepreneurship.

10. Collaboration with AI Industry

Establishing partnerships with AI industry players can provide valuable insights and resources to educational institutions. Industry experts can serve as guest lecturers, mentors, or collaborators on research projects, enhancing the quality of AI education.

In conclusion, preparing students for an AI-driven world is a multifaceted endeavor that involves AI literacy, integration into the curriculum, problem-solving skills, ethical awareness, collaboration, lifelong learning, real-world applications, soft skills, innovation, and industry collaboration. By equipping students with these capabilities, educational institutions can ensure that graduates are well-prepared to thrive in an increasingly AI-powered society.

Here are the chapter and section titles for your book:

Chapter 1: Introduction to Google Bard

- 1.1 The Rise of AI in Search Technology
- 1.2 Understanding Google Bard's Capabilities
- 1.3 The Evolution from Traditional Search Engines to AI-Powered Solutions
- 1.4 Navigating the Interface of Google Bard
- 1.5 Setting Expectations: What Google Bard Can and Cannot Do

Chapter 2: Getting Started with Google Bard

- 2.1 Creating a Google Bard Account
- 2.2 Customizing Your User Experience
- 2.3 Basic and Advanced Search Techniques
- 2.4 Interpreting Google Bard's Responses
- 2.5 Tips for Efficient Information Retrieval

Chapter 3: Advanced Features and Tools

- 3.1 Utilizing Voice Search with Google Bard
- 3.2 Exploring Bard's Interactive Elements

- 3.3 Advanced Query Formulation
- 3.4 Personalization and Privacy Settings
- 3.5 Integrating Google Bard with Other Google Services

Chapter 4: Google Bard in Everyday Life

- 4.1 Enhancing Personal Productivity
- 4.2 Using Google Bard for Educational Purposes
- 4.3 Shopping and Consumer Research
- 4.4 Travel Planning and Local Information
- 4.5 Entertainment and Media Queries

Chapter 5: Business Applications of Google Bard

- 5.1 Market Research and Data Analysis
- 5.2 Enhancing SEO and Digital Marketing
- 5.3 Customer Service and Engagement
- 5.4 Competitive Analysis
- 5.5 Trends Forecasting and Industry Insights

Chapter 6: Understanding AI and Natural Language Processing

- 6.1 The Basics of AI in Search Engines
- 6.2 How Google Bard Processes Language
- 6.3 The Role of Machine Learning
- 6.4 AI Ethics and Responsible Use
- 6.5 Limitations and Challenges of AI in Search

Chapter 7: Google Bard for Content Creators

- 7.1 Researching and Generating Ideas
- 7.2 Analyzing Audience Trends
- 7.3 SEO Optimization for Content
- 7.4 Monitoring Content Performance
- 7.5 Collaborating and Sharing Insights

Chapter 8: Troubleshooting Common Issues

- 8.1 Addressing Search Accuracy Problems
- 8.2 Handling Misunderstandings and Errors
- 8.3 Updating User Preferences and Settings
- 8.4 Reporting Bugs and Providing Feedback
- 8.5 Staying Informed About Updates and Changes

Chapter 9: Privacy and Security with Google Bard

- 9.1 Understanding Data Collection and Use
- 9.2 Managing Your Digital Footprint
- 9.3 Security Features and Protocols
- 9.4 Best Practices for Protecting Personal Information
- 9.5 The Future of Privacy in AI-Powered Search

Chapter 10: Educational Integration of Google Bard

- 10.1 Incorporating Bard into Classroom Learning
- 10.2 Facilitating Research and Study
- 10.3 Encouraging Critical Thinking and Analysis
- 10.4 Balancing Technology and Traditional Learning Methods
- 10.5 Preparing Students for an AI-Driven World

Chapter 11: Social and Cultural Impacts

- 11.1 Google Bard's Influence on Information Consumption
- 11.2 Bridging Cultural and Language Barriers
- 11.3 The Role in Promoting Digital Literacy
- 11.4 Addressing Misinformation and Bias
- 11.5 Fostering Global Knowledge Exchange

Chapter 12: The Future of AI in Search

- 12.1 Current Trends and Innovations
- 12.2 Predicting the Next Steps for Google Bard
- 12.3 The Role of User Feedback in Shaping AI
- 12.4 Ethical Considerations and Future Challenges

- 12.5 Imagining the Long-Term Impact of AI on Information Access

Chapter 13: Tips for Effective Searches

- 13.1 Crafting Precise Search Queries
- 13.2 Utilizing Filters and Advanced Search Options
- 13.3 Deciphering and Evaluating Search Results
- 13.4 Leveraging Google Bard for Complex Queries
- 13.5 Continuous Learning and Adaptation

Chapter 14: Networking and Community Engagement

- 14.1 Connecting with Other Google Bard Users
- 14.2 Participating in Forums and Discussion Groups
- 14.3 Sharing Tips and Best Practices
- 14.4 Collaborative Learning and Support
- 14.5 Building a Community of Informed Users

Chapter 15: Personal Development and Learning

- 15.1 Using Google Bard for Self-Improvement
- 15.2 Lifelong Learning and Skill Development
- 15.3 Exploring Diverse Topics and Interests
- 15.4 Staying Informed and Curious

Chapter 11: Social and Cultural Impacts

11.1 Google Bard's Influence on Information Consumption

In today's digital age, information consumption has undergone a transformative shift, largely influenced by advancements in AI-powered search engines like Google Bard. This section explores how Google Bard has shaped the way people access, interact with, and perceive information in the realms of social and culture.

The Evolution of Information Discovery

Traditionally, individuals relied on libraries, encyclopedias, and printed materials for information. Google Bard, with its ability to provide instant access to a vast repository of knowledge, has revolutionized the process of information discovery. Users can now effortlessly retrieve facts, explanations, and insights on virtually any topic, leading to a democratization of information.

The Role of Personalization

Google Bard's algorithms are designed to tailor search results based on a user's preferences, location, and search history. While this personalization enhances user experience, it also raises questions about filter bubbles and echo chambers. Users may find themselves exposed primarily to information that aligns with their existing beliefs, potentially reinforcing cognitive biases.

Bridging Language and Cultural Barriers

One of Google Bard's remarkable features is its ability to provide search results in multiple languages. This capability fosters cross-cultural communication and knowledge exchange. It enables users to access information from diverse sources worldwide, facilitating a deeper understanding of different cultures and perspectives.

Digital Literacy Promotion

Google Bard plays a significant role in promoting digital literacy. By providing instant access to information, it encourages users to develop critical thinking skills. However, it also presents challenges related to misinformation and disinformation. Users must learn to evaluate sources and verify information to navigate the digital landscape effectively.

Addressing Misinformation and Bias

The proliferation of misinformation and biased content online is a concern in today's information age. Google Bard has implemented measures to combat this issue by prioritizing authoritative sources and fact-checking information. Nevertheless, the battle against misinformation remains an ongoing challenge.

Fostering Global Knowledge Exchange

Through its search capabilities, Google Bard has facilitated global knowledge exchange. Researchers, students, and professionals can collaborate and access information from around the world. This interconnectedness has accelerated progress in various fields, from science to the arts.

In conclusion, Google Bard's influence on information consumption is profound, impacting how individuals discover, personalize, and interact with information. While it offers numerous benefits, it also presents challenges related to personalization, digital literacy, and the spread of misinformation. Understanding these impacts is crucial for individuals and society as a whole as they navigate the ever-evolving landscape of information access and consumption.

11.2 Bridging Cultural and Language Barriers

In a world that is more interconnected than ever, cultural and language barriers have traditionally posed challenges to communication and understanding. Google Bard, as an AI-powered search engine, has played a pivotal role in bridging these gaps and facilitating cross-cultural interaction and collaboration.

Language Translation

One of Google Bard's standout features is its robust language translation capabilities. Users can input queries or text in one language, and Google Bard can provide translations in numerous languages. This feature is invaluable for breaking down language barriers, allowing individuals from different linguistic backgrounds to access and share information effortlessly.

Cultural Insights

Google Bard is not just a language translation tool; it also provides cultural insights. When users search for topics related to specific cultures, regions, or traditions, Google Bard can provide contextual information and explanations, enhancing users' understanding of cultural nuances.

Global Access to Information

Through its vast database of indexed websites, Google Bard provides global access to information. This is particularly important for individuals seeking knowledge about other cultures, world events, or international news. It enables people to stay informed about global affairs and engage in cross-cultural dialogue.

Multilingual Content Creation

For content creators and businesses, Google Bard's language capabilities open up new opportunities. They can create content that appeals to a broader international audience by using translation tools and cultural insights to tailor their messages effectively.

Language Learning

Google Bard can be a valuable companion for language learners. Users can enter phrases or words in their target language to get translations and practice pronunciation using voice search. This aids language acquisition and encourages multiculturalism.

Challenges and Ethical Considerations

While Google Bard's efforts to bridge cultural and language barriers are commendable, they also raise ethical considerations. Machine translation, while useful, may not always capture the nuances and cultural sensitivities of languages. There is also the risk of perpetuating cultural stereotypes or biases through automated translations.

Additionally, there are concerns related to privacy and data security, especially when users input text in languages other than their primary language. Users should be aware of the potential implications of sharing personal or sensitive information through translation tools.

In conclusion, Google Bard's ability to bridge cultural and language barriers has had a significant impact on global communication and understanding. It has facilitated cross-cultural interactions, access to international information, and language learning. However, users and developers must remain vigilant about the ethical considerations and potential challenges associated with these capabilities. As Google Bard continues to evolve, it has the potential to further enhance global connectivity and cultural exchange.

11.3 The Role in Promoting Digital Literacy

Digital literacy is the ability to find, evaluate, and use information effectively, particularly in the context of the digital age. Google Bard plays a significant role in promoting digital literacy by providing users with access to vast amounts of information, tools to verify sources, and resources to improve their digital skills.

Access to Information

Google Bard is a gateway to the internet's vast knowledge repository. It allows users to search for information on a wide range of topics. This accessibility empowers individuals to learn about new subjects, stay informed about current events, and explore various perspectives on issues.

Source Verification

Promoting digital literacy includes the ability to discern reliable sources from unreliable ones. Google Bard offers tools that help users evaluate the credibility of information. For instance, users can access fact-checking resources, view the publication date of web pages, and cross-reference information from multiple sources.

Media Literacy

In an era of digital media, understanding the different forms of media and their impact is crucial. Google Bard provides access to news articles, videos, podcasts, and more. Users can explore different media formats and develop media literacy skills to critically assess the content they encounter.

Online Safety and Security

Digital literacy also encompasses online safety and security. Google Bard educates users about safe online practices and the importance of protecting personal information. It promotes awareness of cybersecurity threats, such as phishing and malware, and encourages users to take appropriate precautions.

Educational Resources

Google Bard offers a multitude of educational resources, including online courses, tutorials, and documentation. These resources support users in acquiring new digital skills, from basic computer proficiency to more advanced subjects like coding and data analysis.

Closing the Digital Divide

One of the challenges in promoting digital literacy is addressing the digital divide, which refers to the gap between individuals who have access to digital technologies and those who do not. Google Bard can help bridge this gap by offering resources that promote digital inclusion and providing access to information for underserved populations.

Challenges in Promoting Digital Literacy

While Google Bard plays a vital role in promoting digital literacy, there are challenges. The internet is a vast space with both reliable and misleading information, making it challenging for users to navigate. The sheer volume of content can be overwhelming, and users may struggle to discern credible sources from misinformation.

Additionally, digital literacy is an ongoing process that requires continuous learning and adaptation. Google Bard can help by providing access to educational materials, but users must take the initiative to improve their digital skills continually.

In conclusion, Google Bard contributes significantly to promoting digital literacy by providing access to information, tools for source verification, and resources for skill development. It empowers users to become more digitally literate and navigate the digital landscape effectively. However, addressing challenges such as misinformation and the digital divide remains an ongoing effort for both users and technology providers.

11.4 Addressing Misinformation and Bias

In the age of information abundance, one of the significant challenges we face is the proliferation of misinformation and bias in digital content. Misinformation refers to false or misleading information shared without malicious intent, while bias involves the unfair or partial representation of facts or perspectives. Google Bard plays a crucial role in addressing these issues by implementing various strategies and features to combat misinformation and bias.

Fact-Checking and Source Verification

Google Bard provides users with tools and resources to fact-check information and verify the credibility of sources. Users can access fact-checking websites, view the publication date of web pages, and assess the reliability of the information they encounter. Encouraging source verification helps users make informed judgments about the content they consume.

Algorithmic Improvements

Google Bard continually updates its search algorithms to prioritize authoritative and trustworthy sources. This helps reduce the visibility of unreliable or low-quality information in search results. Algorithmic improvements aim to surface content from reputable sources and enhance the overall quality of search results.

Diverse Perspectives

To combat bias, Google Bard strives to present a diverse range of perspectives and sources in search results. This inclusivity ensures that users are exposed to a variety of viewpoints, reducing the risk of content that promotes a single narrative or agenda. By promoting diversity, Google Bard helps users develop a more comprehensive understanding of complex issues.

User Feedback Mechanisms

Google Bard actively seeks user feedback to identify and address instances of misinformation and bias. Users can report problematic search results or content, helping the platform improve its algorithms and content ranking. This collaborative approach empowers users to contribute to the quality and integrity of search results.

Transparency Initiatives

To foster transparency, Google Bard shares information about its content ranking processes and algorithmic updates. This transparency allows users to understand how search results are generated and how content is evaluated for quality and relevance. It also helps users hold the platform accountable for its content curation efforts.

Media Literacy Resources

Google Bard offers resources to enhance media literacy skills. These resources educate users on critical thinking, source evaluation, and the recognition of biased or misleading content. By promoting media literacy, Google Bard empowers users to navigate the digital landscape more effectively.

Challenges in Addressing Misinformation and Bias

While Google Bard's efforts to combat misinformation and bias are commendable, challenges remain. The scale of the internet and the volume of content uploaded daily make it challenging to detect and address every instance of misinformation or bias. Additionally, the subjective nature of bias makes it difficult to develop algorithms that can fully eliminate it.

Moreover, addressing these issues requires a delicate balance between content moderation and respecting freedom of expression. Striking the right balance is an ongoing challenge for platforms like Google Bard.

In conclusion, Google Bard takes significant steps to combat misinformation and bias by implementing fact-checking tools, algorithmic improvements, promoting diverse perspectives, seeking user feedback, and offering media literacy resources. While challenges persist, these efforts contribute to a more reliable and informative online environment. Users, too, play a crucial role in critically evaluating content and reporting issues to ensure the continued improvement of digital information quality.

11.5 Fostering Global Knowledge Exchange

In an interconnected world, the internet serves as a powerful tool for fostering global knowledge exchange. Google Bard, as a leading AI-powered search engine, plays a pivotal role in facilitating the dissemination of information and enabling cross-cultural communication. In this section, we'll explore how Google Bard contributes to the exchange of knowledge and ideas on a global scale.

Multilingual Capabilities

One of the key features that make Google Bard a powerful tool for global knowledge exchange is its multilingual capabilities. The search engine supports a vast array of languages, allowing users from different regions and linguistic backgrounds to access information in their preferred language. This inclusivity promotes the sharing of knowledge across borders and cultures.

Access to Diverse Content

Google Bard's search algorithms are designed to provide access to a wide range of content, including articles, research papers, videos, and more. This diversity ensures that users can explore a rich tapestry of knowledge from various sources and formats. It also encourages cross-disciplinary learning and the exchange of ideas from different fields of study.

Breaking Down Language Barriers

Language barriers have traditionally been a significant impediment to global knowledge exchange. However, Google Bard's translation features, such as Google Translate integration, help break down these barriers. Users can translate web pages and content from one language to another, enabling them to access information that was previously inaccessible due to linguistic differences.

Promoting Cultural Exchange

Google Bard's ability to provide information about different cultures, traditions, and historical events promotes cultural exchange. Users can explore content related to various regions, learn about different customs, and gain a deeper understanding of global diversity. This cultural awareness fosters empathy and cooperation in an increasingly interconnected world.

Access to International News and Events

Google Bard serves as a gateway to international news and events, keeping users informed about global developments. Users can access news articles, live updates, and reports from around the world, allowing them to stay connected to current affairs and global issues. This real-time access to information is instrumental in promoting informed global citizenship.

Collaboration and Research

Researchers, scholars, and professionals worldwide rely on Google Bard for collaboration and research. The search engine's vast database of academic papers, journals, and research publications facilitates cross-border collaborations and the sharing of scholarly knowledge. It also serves as a platform for individuals and institutions to disseminate their research findings to a global audience.

Challenges in Global Knowledge Exchange

While Google Bard contributes significantly to global knowledge exchange, challenges persist. The digital divide, which includes disparities in internet access and digital literacy, can limit some individuals' ability to benefit from this exchange fully. Additionally, issues related to online censorship and information control in certain regions can hinder the free flow of knowledge.

Furthermore, the quality and accuracy of information shared globally can vary widely, and users must exercise critical thinking when evaluating sources. The spread of misinformation and bias, discussed in earlier sections, is a concern that affects global knowledge exchange as well.

In conclusion, Google Bard's multilingual capabilities, access to diverse content, breaking down of language barriers, promotion of cultural exchange, access to international news, and support for collaboration and research all contribute to fostering global knowledge exchange. While challenges exist, the internet and platforms like Google Bard continue to be powerful tools for bridging knowledge gaps and promoting cross-cultural understanding in our interconnected world.

12.1 Current Trends and Innovations

The world of AI-powered search is dynamic and constantly evolving, with new trends and innovations shaping the landscape. In this section, we'll explore the current trends and innovations in AI-driven search engines, with a focus on Google Bard.

1. ***Conversational AI***: One of the most prominent trends is the rise of conversational AI. Google Bard and similar search engines are becoming increasingly adept at understanding and responding to natural language queries. Users can engage in more fluid and conversational interactions, making the search experience feel more intuitive and user-friendly.

2. ***Voice Search***: Voice search continues to gain traction as more people use voice-activated devices like smartphones and smart speakers. Google Bard's voice search capabilities allow users to search for information and perform tasks using voice commands, offering convenience and accessibility.

3. ***Personalization***: AI-powered search engines are getting better at personalizing search results based on user preferences, search history, and behavior. This personalization enhances the user experience by delivering more relevant and tailored content.

4. ***Multimodal Search***: Multimodal search involves combining different types of media, such as text, images, and voice, to perform searches. Google Bard is increasingly incorporating multimodal capabilities, enabling users to search using a combination of text and images, for example.

5. ***AI-Generated Content***: AI-driven content generation is on the rise. Search engines like Google Bard can generate responses, summaries, and even create content, such as news articles or product descriptions, based on user queries. This has implications for content creation and automation.

6. ***Responsible AI***: With growing concerns about AI ethics and bias, there is a trend towards responsible AI in search engines. Google Bard and others are implementing measures to reduce bias, provide transparency, and ensure fair and ethical use of AI.

7. **Vertical Search Engines**: *Vertical search engines cater to specific niches or industries. Google Bard is expanding its capabilities to offer vertical search experiences tailored to fields like healthcare, finance, and e-commerce, providing more specialized results.*

8. **AI in Content Recommendations**: *AI-driven recommendations are not limited to search results. Search engines are using AI to recommend content, products, and services to users, enhancing engagement and user satisfaction.*

9. **Augmented Reality (AR) and Visual Search**: *Visual search, powered by AR and AI, allows users to search for information using images or real-world objects. Google Bard's visual search capabilities enable users to explore the world around them in new ways.*

10. **Real-time Information**: *Google Bard and other search engines are improving their ability to provide real-time information, especially in areas like news and events. Users can get up-to-the-minute updates on topics of interest.*

11. **AI in E-commerce**: *E-commerce platforms are leveraging AI-powered search to enhance product recommendations, improve search relevance, and personalize the shopping experience. Google Bard's integration with e-commerce platforms is a testament to this trend.*

12. **Ethical Considerations**: *Ethical AI usage and data privacy are becoming central concerns. Users and regulators are demanding greater transparency, control over personal data, and adherence to ethical principles in AI-powered search engines.*

In conclusion, the current trends and innovations in AI-powered search engines, including Google Bard, are reshaping how we interact with information and technology. These trends reflect a growing emphasis on user-centric, responsible, and personalized AI experiences, with a focus on natural language understanding, multimodal capabilities, and ethical AI practices. As technology continues to advance, we can expect even more exciting developments in the field of AI-driven search.

12.2 Predicting the Next Steps for Google Bard

As we delve into the future of AI in search engines, it's essential to consider the potential directions and developments that Google Bard might take. While predictions in the rapidly evolving field of AI are subject to change, several trends and possibilities stand out as potential next steps for Google Bard and similar AI-driven search engines:

1. **Enhanced Natural Language Understanding**: Google Bard is likely to continue improving its natural language understanding capabilities. This includes better comprehension of context, nuances, and intent in user queries, making interactions with the search engine even more conversational and intuitive.

2. **Improved Multimodal Search**: Multimodal search, which combines text, images, and voice, is expected to become more sophisticated. Google Bard may offer users seamless experiences where they can switch between different modes of interaction effortlessly.

3. **Expanded Language Support**: Google Bard will likely expand its language support to cater to a more global audience. As AI technology advances, it becomes easier to support a wide range of languages and dialects, enhancing accessibility and inclusivity.

4. **AI-Generated Content**: The generation of content by AI is expected to advance. Google Bard may be able to produce more comprehensive and contextually relevant content, such as reports, summaries, and even creative writing, based on user queries.

5. **Deeper Personalization**: Personalization will continue to be a focal point. Google Bard could offer increasingly tailored experiences by learning from user behavior and preferences, providing more relevant search results and recommendations.

6. **Augmented Reality Integration**: With the rise of augmented reality (AR) technology, Google Bard may integrate AR capabilities for enhanced visual and location-based searches. Users might use their smartphones or AR glasses to interact with the world around them in a search context.

7. **Ethical AI and Bias Mitigation**: Addressing ethical concerns and mitigating bias in AI search engines will remain crucial. Google Bard is likely to invest in measures to ensure fairness, transparency, and responsible AI usage.

8. *AI-Driven Knowledge Graphs*: Google Bard may develop more advanced knowledge graphs, enhancing its ability to provide in-depth information and answer complex queries. These knowledge graphs could cover a broader range of topics and domains.

9. *Vertical Specialization*: Vertical search engines catering to specific industries or domains will likely expand. Google Bard may offer specialized search experiences in areas like healthcare, finance, law, and more.

10. *Integration with IoT Devices*: Google Bard's integration with Internet of Things (IoT) devices may grow. Users could seamlessly access information and perform tasks through smart appliances, cars, and other IoT-enabled devices.

11. *AI-Enhanced Collaboration*: Collaboration tools integrated with Google Bard could become more prevalent. AI-driven assistance in content creation, research, and communication may become standard.

12. *Quantum Computing*: As quantum computing technology matures, it may play a role in enhancing the processing power and capabilities of AI search engines like Google Bard, potentially enabling complex computations and searches.

13. *Human-AI Collaboration*: Google Bard might explore ways for users to collaborate with AI systems actively. This could involve users contributing to AI training, fine-tuning models, or co-creating content.

In summary, the future of Google Bard is likely to involve continuous advancements in natural language understanding, personalization, multimodal interactions, and ethical AI practices. As technology evolves and user demands change, Google Bard will adapt to provide increasingly intelligent, user-centric, and responsible search experiences. While predicting the exact path of AI development is challenging, these trends offer a glimpse into the potential next steps for Google Bard and AI-powered search engines.

12.3 The Role of User Feedback in Shaping AI

User feedback plays a pivotal role in shaping the evolution and improvement of AI systems like Google Bard. As AI technologies continue to advance, user insights, opinions, and experiences are invaluable for fine-tuning and enhancing these systems. In this section, we will explore the significance of user feedback and how it contributes to the development of AI-driven search engines.

The Feedback Loop

User feedback creates a continuous feedback loop that allows AI developers and engineers to gain a deeper understanding of how their systems perform in real-world scenarios. This loop typically involves the following stages:

1. **Collection**: Users provide feedback through various channels, such as in-app surveys, feedback forms, and social media. These channels serve as data collection points.

2. **Analysis**: AI systems analyze the feedback data to identify trends, common issues, and user sentiments. Natural language processing (NLP) techniques are often used to extract valuable insights from unstructured text feedback.

3. **Prioritization**: AI developers prioritize feedback based on severity, frequency, and impact on user experience. Critical issues are addressed first to ensure system reliability.

4. **Iterative Development**: Developers use user feedback to inform iterative improvements. This may involve refining

algorithms, enhancing user interfaces, and addressing specific pain points reported by users.

5. **Testing**: The updated AI system undergoes testing to ensure that the changes effectively address user concerns without introducing new issues.

6. **Deployment**: Once tested and validated, the improvements are deployed, and users may notice enhanced performance or new features.

Types of User Feedback

User feedback comes in various forms, each providing unique insights into AI systems like Google Bard:

- **Bug Reports**: Users report technical issues, such as errors, crashes, or unexpected behavior. These reports are crucial for maintaining system stability.

- **Usability Feedback**: Users share their experiences with the system's interface, suggesting improvements in navigation, layout, and overall usability.

- **Content Relevance**: Feedback on the accuracy and relevance of search results helps fine-tune algorithms to provide more meaningful and contextually accurate information.

- **Feature Requests**: Users propose new features or enhancements, guiding the development team in expanding the system's capabilities.

- **Ethical Concerns**: Users may raise concerns about privacy, bias, or ethical considerations related to AI systems, prompting developers to address these issues.

The Evolution of AI Systems

User feedback drives the evolution of AI systems like Google Bard in several ways:

1. **Quality Assurance**: Feedback helps identify and rectify issues that AI developers may not have encountered during testing, ensuring higher reliability and user satisfaction.
2. **Personalization**: Understanding user preferences through feedback enables AI systems to deliver more personalized experiences, enhancing search results and recommendations.
3. **Bias Mitigation**: User feedback can highlight instances of bias in search results or recommendations, prompting developers to adopt measures for bias mitigation.
4. **Feature Development**: Feature requests from users often lead to the introduction of new functionalities that cater to user needs and preferences.
5. **Ethical Improvements**: Addressing ethical concerns raised by users contributes to the responsible development and deployment of AI systems, fostering trust among users.

User-Centric Development

The integration of user feedback ensures that AI systems like Google Bard remain user-centric. Developers actively listen to the needs and concerns of their user base, allowing AI to evolve in ways that directly benefit users. As AI technology continues to advance, the importance of user feedback in shaping the future of AI-driven search engines cannot be overstated. It fosters a collaborative relationship between developers and users, resulting in more intelligent, ethical, and user-friendly AI systems.

12.4 Ethical Considerations and Future Challenges

The rapid advancement of AI, particularly in search engines like Google Bard, brings forth a host of ethical considerations and challenges. In this section, we delve into these important aspects that AI developers and users must navigate in the quest for responsible AI technology.

Transparency and Explainability

One of the foremost ethical concerns in AI is the lack of transparency and explainability. AI systems, especially deep learning models, often function as black boxes, making it challenging to understand how they arrive at particular decisions or recommendations. This opacity raises questions about accountability and trustworthiness. Developers are increasingly focusing on creating more interpretable AI models and providing explanations for AI-driven outcomes.

Bias and Fairness

Bias in AI algorithms is a pervasive issue. AI systems can inadvertently learn biases present in training data, leading to discriminatory or unfair outcomes. Addressing bias and ensuring fairness in AI-powered search engines is paramount. Developers are actively working on bias detection and mitigation techniques, while also diversifying training data to reduce bias.

Privacy and Data Protection

AI systems like Google Bard rely on vast amounts of user data to provide personalized experiences. However, this dependence on user data poses significant privacy concerns. Striking a balance between personalization and data protection is a persistent challenge. Future developments in AI will likely involve stronger data anonymization, user control over data usage, and stricter privacy regulations.

Algorithmic Accountability

As AI systems take on more critical roles in decision-making, the need for algorithmic accountability becomes crucial. Users should have a clear understanding of how algorithms make decisions and the ability to challenge those decisions. Developing standards for algorithmic accountability and user recourse mechanisms is an ongoing endeavor.

Socioeconomic Impact

AI's impact on employment and the workforce is a multifaceted issue. While AI can boost productivity and create new job opportunities, it can also lead to job displacement. Preparing the workforce for an AI-driven future and addressing the socioeconomic consequences of AI are key challenges.

Environmental Sustainability

The energy consumption of large-scale AI models, often powered by data centers, raises concerns about environmental sustainability. Finding energy-efficient AI solutions and reducing the carbon footprint of AI infrastructure are pressing challenges.

International Regulations and Governance

AI transcends national borders, necessitating international cooperation and regulations to address ethical and legal considerations consistently. Crafting global standards for AI ethics, data sharing, and responsible AI development is an ongoing endeavor.

Ethical User Education

Users of AI systems need to be educated about the ethical implications and limitations of AI. Ethical user education is vital for fostering responsible AI usage and encouraging users to provide constructive feedback when they encounter issues.

Future Challenges and Collaborative Solutions

The ethical considerations surrounding AI will continue to evolve as technology advances. Addressing these challenges requires a collaborative effort involving AI developers, policymakers, ethicists, researchers, and users. Open dialogue, transparency, and proactive measures are essential to ensure that AI, including AI-powered search engines like Google Bard, benefits society while upholding ethical standards.

As we look to the future, responsible AI development and ethical AI usage will remain at the forefront of discussions and actions, shaping the direction of AI technology in search engines and beyond.

12.5 Imagining the Long-Term Impact of AI on Information Access

As we peer into the future, it becomes evident that AI, including AI-powered search engines like Google Bard, will have a profound and lasting impact on how we access and interact with information. This section explores the long-term implications and potential scenarios for AI in information retrieval.

Enhanced Information Retrieval

In the coming years, AI will continue to advance information retrieval capabilities. AI-powered search engines will become even more adept at understanding user intent, context, and nuances in queries. Natural language processing (NLP) models will evolve to the point where they can handle complex, conversational queries effectively.

Personalization and Hyper-Personalization

AI will enable hyper-personalization of search results and content recommendations. Search engines will understand users on a deeply individual level, delivering content tailored not only to preferences but also to emotional states and real-time needs. This will revolutionize content consumption and user experiences.

AI-Augmented Creativity

AI tools will become indispensable for content creators, writers, artists, and musicians. They will assist in generating ideas, fine-tuning content, and automating repetitive tasks, freeing creators to focus on higher-level creativity. AI-generated content will coexist with human-created content seamlessly.

Ethical and Bias-Free AI

Ethical considerations will be ingrained in AI development. Bias detection and mitigation will be standard practice, ensuring fairness in search results and recommendations. AI will be held to higher standards of transparency and accountability, with mechanisms for addressing algorithmic decisions.

AI-Powered Education

AI will play an increasingly prominent role in education. Personalized learning experiences, intelligent tutoring systems, and AI-driven assessments will reshape how students learn and educators teach. AI will adapt to diverse learning styles and support lifelong learning.

Global Access to Information

AI-powered translation and multilingual capabilities will break language barriers, granting global access to information in diverse languages. This will foster cross-cultural understanding and democratize access to knowledge.

Sustainable AI

Environmental concerns will drive the development of energy-efficient AI models and data centers. AI will be harnessed to address sustainability challenges, from optimizing energy consumption to aiding environmental research.

Human-AI Collaboration

The future will see enhanced collaboration between humans and AI. AI will provide valuable insights and recommendations, augmenting human decision-making in various fields, from healthcare diagnosis to scientific research.

AI Ethics and Governance

AI governance will be a global concern. International agreements and frameworks will be established to address ethical, legal, and policy aspects of AI. Ethical guidelines for AI development and usage will be refined and adhered to more rigorously.

Continuous Learning and Adaptation

AI systems will continuously learn and adapt to evolving user needs and preferences. They will actively seek user feedback and adapt in real time, ensuring that search results and recommendations remain relevant and up to date.

As we venture further into the AI-driven era of information access, the possibilities are vast, but so are the responsibilities. Striking a balance between harnessing AI's potential for enhancing information access and safeguarding ethical and societal concerns will be an ongoing endeavor. The future of AI in information retrieval promises an exciting and transformative journey, where innovation and ethical considerations walk hand in hand.

13.1 Crafting Precise Search Queries

In the ever-expanding digital landscape, the ability to craft precise search queries is a valuable skill. Whether you are a student researching a topic, a professional seeking information, or someone looking for answers to everyday questions, knowing how to formulate effective search queries can significantly enhance your search experience. This section delves into the art and science of crafting precise search queries to yield accurate and relevant results.

Understanding the Basics

Before delving into advanced techniques, it's crucial to grasp the fundamentals of search queries. Search engines like Google Bard rely on keywords and phrases to retrieve information from vast databases. Here are some key concepts to keep in mind:

- **Keywords:** These are the words or phrases you enter into a search engine to find information. For example, if you're looking for information about climate change, "climate change" would be your primary keyword.

- **Boolean Operators:** These are words that help refine your search. Common Boolean operators include "AND," "OR," and "NOT." For instance, using "AND" between two keywords narrows down results to pages that contain both keywords.

- **Quotation Marks:** Placing quotation marks around a phrase instructs the search engine to look for that exact phrase. For example, searching for "renewable energy sources" will prioritize results containing that exact phrase.

Specificity Matters

The more specific your query, the more relevant your results are likely to be. Consider the following tips:

1. **Use Descriptive Keywords:** Instead of vague terms, use descriptive keywords that precisely represent what you're looking for. For instance, instead of searching for "cars," you might search for "electric hybrid cars."

2. **Include Context:** Provide additional context or qualifiers to narrow down your search. For example, if you're interested in recent developments in artificial intelligence, you can add "2023" to your query.

3. **Eliminate Unnecessary Words:** Avoid using common words like "how," "what," or "the" in your query, as they can dilute its specificity. Focus on the essential keywords.

Boolean Logic for Precision

Understanding Boolean operators can greatly enhance your search:

- **AND:** Use "AND" to require that both keywords are present in the results. For instance, "machine learning AND healthcare" ensures results related to both topics.

- **OR:** Use "OR" to broaden your search. "Machine learning OR artificial intelligence" will retrieve results related to either topic.

- **NOT:** Use "NOT" to exclude specific keywords. If you're interested in machine learning but want to exclude information about deep learning, you can search for "machine learning NOT deep learning."

Advanced Query Techniques

For more advanced users, consider these techniques:

- **Wildcard (*):** The asterisk can substitute for any number of characters. "Genetic * research" will return results related to genetic engineering, genetic testing, and more.

- **Site Search:** Limit your search to a specific website by using "site:" followed by the domain. For example, "site:wikipedia.org artificial intelligence" will only show results from Wikipedia.

- **File Type:** To find specific file types, add "filetype:" followed by the file extension. "Machine learning filetype:pdf" will retrieve PDF documents related to machine learning.

- **Synonyms (~):** The tilde (~) operator can help include synonyms in your search. " ~automobile" will return results related to cars, vehicles, and other similar terms.

Crafting precise search queries is an iterative process. Don't be afraid to experiment and refine your queries as you explore search results. With practice, you can become a more proficient searcher, saving time and finding the information you need more effectively.

13.2 Utilizing Filters and Advanced Search Options

In your quest for precise and relevant search results, utilizing filters and advanced search options can be a game-changer. While crafting effective queries (as discussed in the previous section) is essential, applying filters and leveraging advanced search capabilities can help you fine-tune your search results further. This section explores how to use filters and advanced options in search engines like Google Bard to streamline your information retrieval process.

The Power of Filters

Filters are pre-defined criteria that allow you to narrow down search results based on specific attributes. While the available filters may vary depending on the search engine you're using, here are some common filter categories and how to use them:

1. **Time-Based Filters:** These filters enable you to specify a time range for your search results. For instance, you can filter results to show only those from the past year,

month, or a custom date range. This is particularly useful when you're looking for up-to-date information.

2. **File Type Filters:** If you're searching for specific types of files, such as PDFs or PowerPoint presentations, you can use file type filters. This ensures that your results include only the file formats you're interested in.

3. **Language Filters:** If you prefer results in a specific language, language filters can help. You can specify the language in which you want the content to be displayed.

4. **Location Filters:** For location-specific information, you can use location filters. These filters allow you to restrict results to a particular region or country.

5. **Usage Rights Filters:** When you're looking for content that you can reuse, modify, or share, usage rights filters come in handy. They help you find content with specific usage permissions, such as "Creative Commons."

Advanced Search Operators

Beyond filters, search engines often support advanced search operators that give you precise control over your queries. Here are some useful advanced search operators:

- **"site:" Operator:** Use "site:" followed by a domain name to limit your search to a specific website. For example, "site:wikipedia.org artificial intelligence" will only show results from Wikipedia related to artificial intelligence.

- **"intitle:" and "inurl:" Operators:** The "intitle:" operator restricts results to pages with the specified keyword(s) in their title. Similarly, "inurl:" limits results to URLs containing the keyword(s).

- **"related:" Operator:** This operator allows you to find websites related to a specified URL. For instance, "related:nytimes.com" will provide a list of websites related to The New York Times.

- **"define:" Operator:** To get a quick definition of a term, use "define:" followed by the word you want to define. For example, "define:algorithm" will provide a definition of the term "algorithm."

- **"info:" Operator:** To retrieve information about a website, use "info:" followed by the website's URL. This can provide details about the site's traffic, similar sites, and more.

Using Filters and Advanced Options Effectively

To make the most of filters and advanced search options:

1. **Start with a Well-Crafted Query:** Before applying filters, ensure that your initial query is clear and specific. Filters work best when they complement a precise query.

2. **Explore the Options:** Familiarize yourself with the available filters and advanced operators in the search engine you're using. Each search engine may have unique features.

3. **Combine Filters and Operators:** Don't hesitate to combine filters and advanced search operators to refine your results further. For instance, you can use the "site:" operator in conjunction with a time-based filter.

4. **Experiment and Learn:** Like crafting queries, using filters and advanced options is an iterative process. Experiment, observe the results, and learn from your searches to become a more effective searcher.

By mastering filters and advanced search options, you can navigate the vast sea of digital information with greater precision. Whether you're conducting research, seeking specific content types, or aiming to find the most recent information, these tools can help you tailor your searches to your exact needs.

13.3 Deciphering and Evaluating Search Results

Once you've entered your query and applied filters or advanced search options, search engines like Google Bard provide you with a list of search results. However, the mere presence of results doesn't guarantee that you've found exactly what you were looking for. This section explores the critical skill of deciphering and evaluating search results to ensure they meet your information needs.

Understanding Search Snippets

Search results typically consist of a list of web page titles, brief descriptions (known as snippets), and URLs. To evaluate whether a result is relevant to your query, here's what you should look for in a search snippet:

1. **Title:** The title should contain keywords related to your query. It's the first indicator of a page's relevance.

2. **Snippet:** The snippet provides a concise summary of the page's content. It should contain relevant information that matches your query. Look for the appearance of your keywords.

3. **URL:** The URL can provide additional context. It may indicate the source's credibility or relevance to your query. Look for authoritative domains and trusted sources.

Evaluating Relevance and Credibility

To assess the relevance and credibility of search results, consider the following factors:

1. **Relevance to Query:** Does the search result align with your query's intent and keywords? The more closely it matches, the more relevant it is likely to be.

2. **Source Credibility:** Evaluate the source's credibility. Is it from a reputable website or organization? Academic institutions, government sites, and established news outlets often provide reliable information.

3. **Publication Date:** Check the publication date, especially for time-sensitive topics. Recent information may be more relevant, while older content may still have value for historical context.

4. **Authorship:** Determine if there's an identifiable author or organization responsible for the content. Authors with expertise in the subject matter add credibility.

5. **Consistency with Multiple Sources:** Cross-reference information with multiple sources. Consistency across different reputable sources enhances credibility.

6. **User Reviews and Comments:** If available, read user reviews or comments on the page. They can provide insights into the quality and relevance of the content.

Clicking and Exploring

Don't hesitate to click on search results to explore the full content of a page. Often, the snippet provides only a glimpse of what a webpage contains. By visiting the page directly, you can:

- Access in-depth information that may not be summarized in the snippet.
- Evaluate the overall quality of the content, including its organization and readability.
- Determine if the page includes references or citations to other reputable sources.

Using Advanced Search Features

Search engines offer advanced features to further refine your search results. For instance, Google Bard provides options like "Cached" (to view a snapshot of the page as it appeared when indexed) and "Similar" (to find pages similar to the one you're viewing).

Honing Your Evaluation Skills

Deciphering and evaluating search results is a skill that improves with practice. As you conduct more searches and explore various topics, you'll become more adept at quickly assessing the relevance and credibility of search results. Additionally, staying curious, critical, and discerning will serve you well in the digital age, where information is abundant but not always reliable.

13.4 Leveraging Google Bard for Complex Queries

Google Bard, as a sophisticated AI-powered search engine, offers users the ability to perform complex queries that go beyond simple keyword searches. In this section, we'll explore advanced techniques and strategies to help you leverage Google Bard's capabilities for complex queries.

Boolean Operators

One of the fundamental tools for complex queries is the use of Boolean operators. These operators allow you to combine keywords and phrases to refine your search. Here are the main Boolean operators you can use with Google Bard:

- **AND:** This operator narrows your search by requiring all terms to be present in the results. For example, searching for "machine learning AND natural language processing" will return results that include both of these terms.

- **OR:** OR broadens your search by finding results that include either of the terms. For instance, "AI OR artificial intelligence" will return results related to either AI or artificial intelligence.

- **NOT:** NOT excludes specific terms from your search results. If you want to find information about pandas but not the animal, you can search for "pandas NOT animal."

Phrase Searching

To find exact phrases, enclose them in double quotation marks. This ensures that Google Bard looks for the exact phrase rather than individual words. For example, searching for "climate change mitigation strategies" will return results with that specific phrase.

Site and Domain-Specific Searches

You can limit your search to specific websites or domains using the "site:" operator. For instance, "site:wikipedia.org AI" will only return results from Wikipedia related to AI. This is helpful for finding information from trusted sources.

Advanced Search Filters

Google Bard provides advanced search filters that allow you to narrow down results by various criteria, including:

- **File Type:** You can specify the file type you're looking for, such as PDFs, Word documents, or images.

- **Date:** Filter results by a specific date range to find recent or historical information.

- **Location:** If you're interested in local information, you can specify a location to tailor your results.

- **Usage Rights:** Find content that you can reuse for commercial or non-commercial purposes by selecting the appropriate usage rights filter.

Using Wildcards

When you're uncertain about specific terms or want to capture variations, you can use wildcards. An asterisk (*) serves as a wildcard to represent any word or phrase. For example, "AI * ethics" will return results related to AI and various aspects of ethics.

Exploring Related Searches

Google Bard also provides "related searches" at the bottom of the search results page. These suggestions can help you discover additional topics or refine your query for more relevant results.

Combining Techniques

To perform even more advanced searches, you can combine these techniques. For example, you could search for "machine learning AND (natural language processing OR computer vision) site:stanford.edu" to find academic resources on machine learning related to either natural language processing or computer vision from Stanford University's website.

By mastering these advanced search techniques, you can harness the full power of Google Bard to find precise, relevant, and comprehensive information on a wide range of topics.

13.5 Continuous Learning and Adaptation

In the fast-paced world of AI-powered search engines and information retrieval, the key to success is continuous learning and adaptation. Google Bard, like other AI technologies, is constantly evolving, and users must stay informed and adapt their search strategies to make the most of its capabilities.

Staying Informed

1. **Official Documentation:** The first step in continuous learning is to consult the official documentation provided by Google Bard. This documentation is regularly updated and contains valuable information about new features, changes, and best practices.

2. **Blogs and News:** Many tech blogs and news outlets cover updates and developments related to AI and search engines. Following reputable sources can keep you informed about the latest trends and innovations.

3. **User Communities:** Joining online user communities or forums dedicated to Google Bard can be immensely beneficial. Here, users share tips, discuss experiences, and often have inside information about updates or hidden features.

4. **Newsletters:** Consider subscribing to newsletters or mailing lists related to AI, natural language processing, or search technology. These newsletters often curate and deliver the latest news and insights directly to your inbox.

Experimentation and Adaptation

1. **Experiment with Queries:** Don't be afraid to experiment with different types of queries and search techniques. Trying out various approaches will help you understand how Google Bard interprets and responds to different inputs.

2. **Feedback and User Input:** If you encounter issues or have suggestions for improvement, provide feedback to Google Bard's development team. Your input can contribute to the refinement of the search engine.

3. **AI-Driven Suggestions:** Google Bard's AI-driven suggestions and autocomplete features can help you refine your queries. Pay attention to the suggestions as you type, as they can lead you to more precise results.

4. **User Preferences:** Explore and adapt your user preferences within Google Bard. Customizing settings like search history, location, and privacy options can enhance your search experience.

5. **Stay Ethical:** As AI technologies advance, ethical considerations become more critical. Stay informed about

AI ethics and responsible use to ensure you're using Google Bard in an ethical and responsible manner.

Lifelong Learning

1. **Online Courses:** Consider enrolling in online courses or webinars that cover AI, natural language processing, and information retrieval. Many platforms offer courses that can help you deepen your understanding of these topics.

2. **Books and Publications:** Books and academic publications on AI and search technology provide in-depth knowledge. Reading these materials can be a valuable source of continuous learning.

3. **Networking:** Networking with professionals in the AI and search industry can provide insights and opportunities for collaboration. Attend conferences, webinars, and meetups to expand your network.

4. **Teaching and Sharing:** Teaching others what you've learned is an effective way to solidify your knowledge. Consider sharing your expertise through blogs, tutorials, or by mentoring others interested in AI and search.

5. **Lifelong Curiosity:** Finally, maintain your curiosity and passion for learning. The field of AI and search technology is continually evolving, and staying curious will drive your continuous learning journey.

In conclusion, continuous learning and adaptation are essential for making the most of Google Bard and other AI-powered search engines. By staying informed, experimenting, and maintaining a lifelong learning mindset, you can navigate the evolving landscape of AI-driven information retrieval effectively.

14.1 Connecting with Other Google Bard Users

One of the valuable aspects of using Google Bard is the opportunity to connect with a community of users who share a common interest in harnessing the power of AI-powered search. This section explores the benefits of connecting with other Google Bard users, whether it's for learning, problem-solving, or simply sharing your insights and experiences.

Joining Online Forums and Communities

1. **Google Bard Subreddit:** Reddit is home to a dedicated Google Bard community where users discuss tips, tricks, and challenges they encounter. Joining this subreddit allows you to engage in conversations, ask questions, and stay updated on the latest developments.

2. **Tech Forums:** Many tech-related forums have sections dedicated to AI, search engines, and machine learning. Participating in these forums can help you broaden your knowledge and connect with experts in the field.

3. **Social Media Groups:** Platforms like Facebook and LinkedIn host groups focused on AI and search technology. These groups often feature discussions, webinars, and networking opportunities.

Benefits of Community Engagement

1. **Problem Solving:** When you encounter issues or challenges while using Google Bard, reaching out to the community can be a valuable resource. Experienced users may offer solutions or workarounds.

2. **Learning and Sharing:** Engaging with other users allows you to learn from their experiences and share your own insights. It's a two-way street where everyone benefits from collective knowledge.

3. **Staying Informed:** Community members often share news, updates, and hidden features related to Google

Bard. By participating, you can stay informed about the latest developments.

4. **Networking:** Building connections in the AI and search industry can lead to opportunities for collaboration, career growth, and partnerships. You might find like-minded individuals or potential mentors.

Tips for Effective Engagement

1. **Respect Others:** Be respectful and considerate in your interactions with the community. Even if you disagree with someone, maintain a civil and constructive tone.

2. **Contribute Meaningfully:** Share your experiences, insights, and expertise. Meaningful contributions enrich the community and make it a valuable resource for all.

3. **Ask Questions Thoughtfully:** When asking questions, provide context and details. Clear, well-formulated questions are more likely to receive helpful responses.

4. **Use Proper Etiquette:** Familiarize yourself with the etiquette and rules of the specific community or forum you join. Each platform may have its own guidelines.

5. **Stay Informed:** Keep up with the discussions, and if you find a solution to a problem you previously asked about, consider sharing it with the community to help others.

6. **Network Genuinely:** Don't approach networking solely as a means to an end. Build genuine connections, as they can lead to valuable relationships.

Remember that community engagement is a two-way street. By actively participating and contributing to the Google Bard user community, you not only enhance your own knowledge and problem-solving abilities but also help create a more vibrant and supportive ecosystem for everyone.

14.2 Participating in Forums and Discussion Groups

For users of Google Bard, participating in online forums and discussion groups can be a valuable way to expand your knowledge, find solutions to problems, and engage with a community of like-minded individuals. In this section, we'll explore the benefits of participating in such forums and provide some tips for making the most of your engagement.

Benefits of Forum Participation

1. **Knowledge Sharing:** Online forums and discussion groups are treasure troves of information. You can find answers to common questions, learn from others' experiences, and discover new tips and tricks for using Google Bard effectively.

2. **Problem Solving:** If you encounter challenges or technical issues while using Google Bard, these platforms provide a space to seek help. Knowledgeable community members often offer solutions or guidance.

3. **Networking:** Forums and discussion groups connect you with a diverse group of users who share your interest in Google Bard. This can lead to valuable professional connections, collaborations, and even job opportunities.

4. **Staying Informed:** Google Bard and AI-related forums often feature discussions about the latest updates, features, and trends in the field. Staying engaged keeps you informed about the evolving landscape.

Finding the Right Forums

1. **Official Google Bard Community:** Start by exploring Google's official community or support forum for Google Bard. It's an excellent place to seek help, report issues, and stay updated on official announcements.

2. **AI and Machine Learning Forums:** Look for forums and groups dedicated to AI, machine learning, and natural language processing. These communities often have sections or discussions related to Google Bard.

3. **Tech and Webmaster Forums:** Consider tech-related forums that cover topics like search engines, web development, and digital marketing. Google Bard's impact on SEO and online marketing is a common discussion point.

4. **Social Media Groups:** Platforms like Reddit, Facebook, and LinkedIn host groups or subreddits focused on AI and technology. Joining these groups can expand your network.

Tips for Effective Participation

1. **Read Guidelines:** Familiarize yourself with the rules and guidelines of the forum or group you join. Different platforms have varying etiquette and posting requirements.

2. **Search Before You Post:** Before asking a question, use the forum's search feature to see if your issue has already been addressed. Duplicate questions can clutter the forum.

3. **Be Specific:** When seeking help or sharing insights, provide clear and specific details. This makes it easier for others to understand your situation and offer relevant responses.

4. **Contribute Positively:** Actively engage in discussions, offer solutions, and share your knowledge when you can. Positive contributions enrich the community.

5. **Respect Others:** Maintain a respectful and professional tone in your interactions. Disagreements can happen, but it's essential to keep discussions civil.

6. **Stay Active:** Regularly check the forums for new discussions, questions, and updates. Staying active ensures that you continue to benefit from the community.

7. **Protect Your Privacy:** Be cautious about sharing personal or sensitive information in public forums. Use private messages or email when necessary.

Participating in forums and discussion groups can be a rewarding experience for Google Bard users. Whether you're seeking solutions to challenges or looking to share your expertise, these communities offer a platform for meaningful engagement and learning.

14.3 Sharing Tips and Best Practices

One of the key advantages of participating in forums and discussion groups related to Google Bard is the opportunity to share valuable tips and best practices with the community. In this section, we'll delve into the importance of sharing your insights and how to effectively contribute to these platforms.

Why Share Tips and Best Practices?

1. **Community Growth:** Sharing your knowledge benefits the entire community by helping others solve problems, learn new techniques, and improve their use of Google Bard.

2. **Reciprocity:** By contributing tips and best practices, you're more likely to receive help and insights when you need them. It's a give-and-take relationship within the community.

3. **Professional Development:** Sharing your expertise enhances your reputation within the community and the

industry. It can open up opportunities for networking and collaboration.

4. **Staying Updated:** Discussing best practices often leads to discussions about the latest trends and features. It keeps you informed about Google Bard's evolving capabilities.

Effective Tip Sharing

1. **Clarity:** When sharing a tip or best practice, ensure that it's clear, concise, and easy to follow. Use step-by-step instructions if applicable.

2. **Real-Life Examples:** Whenever possible, provide real-life examples or scenarios where your tip has been beneficial. This helps others understand the practical application.

3. **Relevance:** Tailor your tips to the specific needs and interests of the community. Consider the level of expertise of the audience and adjust your tips accordingly.

4. **Engage in Discussions:** Don't just drop tips and disappear. Engage in discussions related to your tip. Answer questions and provide additional context if needed.

Best Practices for Contribution

1. **Start Discussions:** Don't wait for others to initiate discussions. If you have a topic or question related to Google Bard that hasn't been addressed, feel free to start a new thread.

2. **Quality Over Quantity:** It's not about how many posts you make, but the quality of your contributions. Provide valuable insights rather than spamming the forum with low-quality content.

3. **Respect Other Opinions:** While sharing your tips and best practices, respect the opinions and experiences of

others. Constructive criticism is welcome, but avoid being confrontational.

4. **Cite Sources:** If you're sharing information from external sources, cite them appropriately. This adds credibility to your contributions.

Encouraging Discussion

Encouraging discussion around your tips and best practices can lead to a richer learning experience for everyone involved. Here are some strategies to foster engagement:

1. **Ask Questions:** Pose questions related to your tip to stimulate discussion. Encourage others to share their experiences and variations.

2. **Seek Feedback:** Be open to feedback on your tips. Others may have suggestions for improvement or additional insights.

3. **Acknowledge Contributions:** When others contribute to the discussion around your tip, acknowledge their input and express appreciation.

4. **Highlight Success Stories:** Share success stories from community members who have applied your tips. This motivates others to try your recommendations.

In conclusion, sharing tips and best practices in forums and discussion groups related to Google Bard can be a mutually beneficial endeavor. It contributes to the growth of the community, enhances your professional development, and keeps you informed about the latest trends in AI-powered search technology. By following best practices for contribution and encouraging discussions, you can make a meaningful impact within these communities.

14.4 Collaborative Learning and Support

Collaborative learning and support play a crucial role in forums and discussion groups dedicated to Google Bard. These platforms provide a unique space where users can come together to help each other learn, troubleshoot issues, and explore innovative ways to leverage Google Bard's capabilities. In this section, we'll explore the significance of collaborative learning and how to effectively seek and offer support within these communities.

The Power of Collaborative Learning

1. **Diverse Perspectives:** Collaborative learning brings together individuals with diverse backgrounds, experiences, and expertise. This diversity enriches discussions and exposes users to various approaches and solutions.

2. **Collective Problem Solving:** When you encounter challenges or questions related to Google Bard, the collective intelligence of the community can often provide faster and more effective solutions than individual efforts.

3. **Peer Support:** Collaborative learning environments create a supportive atmosphere where users feel comfortable asking questions and seeking help without fear of judgment.

4. **Skill Enhancement:** Active participation in discussions and helping others can enhance your own knowledge and skills. Explaining concepts to others reinforces your understanding.

Effective Collaboration and Support

To make the most of collaborative learning and support within Google Bard communities, consider the following strategies:

Seeking Support:
1. **Clear Communication:** When seeking help, provide clear and concise descriptions of your issues or questions. Include relevant details such as error messages or steps you've already taken.

2. **Search Before Posting:** Before creating a new post, search the forum or group to see if your question has already been answered. This avoids redundancy and helps you find solutions faster.

3. **Engage Actively:** After posting your question, actively engage with responses and provide additional information if requested. This helps others understand your problem better.

4. **Be Patient and Grateful:** Remember that community members are volunteering their time to assist you. Be patient and express gratitude for their help.

Offering Support:
1. **Empathetic Responses:** When responding to others' questions or issues, show empathy and understanding. Avoid condescension or frustration, even if the question seems basic.

2. **Provide Detailed Solutions:** If you can help, provide detailed solutions or step-by-step instructions. Screenshots or code snippets can be immensely helpful.

3. **Ask for Clarifications:** If a user's question is unclear, politely ask for clarifications to ensure you fully understand the problem before offering assistance.

4. **Point to Resources:** Direct users to relevant documentation or resources if their question can be answered through self-help materials.

Building a Supportive Community

To foster a supportive and collaborative learning environment within Google Bard forums and discussion groups, community members can take the following actions:

1. **Moderation and Enforcement:** Moderators can enforce community guidelines to ensure respectful and constructive interactions. They can also facilitate discussions and organize events.

2. **Organize Workshops and Webinars:** Hosting virtual workshops or webinars on specific Google Bard topics can facilitate deeper learning and skill development among members.

3. **Recognize Contributions:** Acknowledge and celebrate the contributions of active and helpful community members. This can inspire others to participate more actively.

4. **Encourage Feedback:** Encourage members to provide feedback on the community's effectiveness and suggest improvements. This helps evolve the community in a positive direction.

In conclusion, collaborative learning and support are integral components of Google Bard communities. They empower users to learn from each other, solve problems together, and collectively harness the potential of AI-powered search technology. By seeking and offering support effectively, users can create a vibrant and mutually beneficial community that enhances everyone's Google Bard experience.

14.5 Building a Community of Informed Users

Building a community of informed users is a pivotal aspect of the Google Bard ecosystem. This section delves into the importance of creating and nurturing such communities, whether they are forums, social media groups, or dedicated websites. These communities serve as hubs for sharing knowledge, discussing best practices, and staying up-to-date with the latest developments in the world of Google Bard.

The Significance of Informed User Communities

1. **Knowledge Sharing:** Informed user communities are repositories of knowledge. Users share tips, tricks, and solutions, creating a valuable resource for beginners and experienced users alike.

2. **Problem Solving:** When users encounter challenges or issues with Google Bard, these communities provide a space to seek help and collectively find solutions. Often, community members have faced similar problems and can offer guidance.

3. **Staying Updated:** Google Bard is continuously evolving, with updates and new features rolling out regularly. Informed user communities help users stay informed about these changes and understand how to leverage them.

4. **Networking:** These communities facilitate networking and collaboration among users, fostering connections that can lead to fruitful partnerships, projects, or simply friendships.

5. **Feedback Loop:** Informed user communities serve as a feedback loop to Google Bard developers and teams. Users can voice their opinions, report bugs, and suggest improvements, influencing the platform's direction.

Tips for Building and Nurturing Informed User Communities

If you're interested in creating or managing a community of informed Google Bard users, consider these strategies:

1. *Clear Purpose and Guidelines:*
    - Define the community's purpose and goals.
    - Establish clear guidelines for respectful and constructive interactions.
    - Communicate these guidelines to members and enforce them consistently.

2. *Diverse Membership:*
    - Encourage users with varying levels of expertise to join.
    - Embrace diversity in terms of backgrounds, interests, and geographic locations.
    - A diverse community offers a broader range of perspectives.

3. *Quality Content and Discussions:*
    - Promote high-quality content and discussions.
    - Encourage members to share valuable insights, tips, and best practices.
    - Recognize and celebrate well-thought-out contributions.

4. *Knowledge Sharing:*
    - Encourage knowledge sharing through tutorials, guides, and informative posts.
    - Organize Q&A sessions or expert talks to share in-depth knowledge.
    - Foster an environment where users feel motivated to help and educate each other.

5. *Moderation and Engagement:*
    - Appoint moderators to oversee discussions and maintain a positive atmosphere.
    - Encourage community engagement through polls, challenges, or events.

- Respond promptly to user inquiries and feedback.

6. *Feedback Channels:*
- Create channels for users to provide feedback and suggestions.
- Ensure that user feedback is considered and, when feasible, implemented.
- Communicate updates and changes based on user input.

7. *Accessibility:*
- Ensure that the community platform is accessible to all users, including those with disabilities.
- Provide resources and assistance for newcomers to navigate the community effectively.

8. *Recognition and Rewards:*
- Acknowledge and reward active and helpful members.
- Implement a system for badges, titles, or other forms of recognition.
- Recognizing contributions motivates users to stay engaged.

9. *Transparency:*
- Maintain transparency in community management and decision-making.
- Communicate openly about community policies, changes, and future plans.

10. *Evolution and Growth:*
- Be open to evolving the community based on user needs and preferences.
- Consider expanding into new platforms or formats if it aligns with the community's goals.

In summary, building a community of informed Google Bard users is a dynamic process that requires dedication, effective communication, and a commitment to providing value to members. These communities contribute significantly to the growth and improvement of Google Bard by fostering collaboration, knowledge sharing, and a sense of belonging among its users.

Chapter 15: Personal Development and Learning

15.1 Using Google Bard for Self-Improvement

In the age of information and digital connectivity, personal development and continuous learning have become more accessible than ever before. Google Bard serves as an indispensable tool for individuals looking to enhance various aspects of their lives, from acquiring new skills to fostering personal growth. This section explores how you can leverage Google Bard as a catalyst for self-improvement and lifelong learning.

Self-Improvement and Lifelong Learning

1. Access to a World of Knowledge:

Google Bard grants you access to an extensive repository of information. Whether you want to learn a new language, acquire coding skills, or explore philosophy, the answers are just a few keystrokes away.

2. Learning at Your Own Pace:

Unlike traditional learning environments, Google Bard allows you to learn at your own pace. You can delve into subjects that interest you without the pressure of deadlines or structured curricula.

3. Tailored Learning:

Google Bard's AI capabilities enable personalized learning experiences. As you interact with the platform, it adapts to your preferences and provides content tailored to your interests.

4. Skill Development:

If you're aiming to acquire specific skills, Google Bard can guide you through the process. Whether it's programming, cooking, or playing a musical instrument, you can find tutorials, videos, and resources to get started.

5. *Stay Informed:*

Staying informed about current events, trends, and developments is crucial in today's fast-paced world. Google Bard can help you access the latest news, articles, and analysis on topics that matter to you.

Practical Tips for Self-Improvement with Google Bard

To make the most of Google Bard for self-improvement, consider these strategies:

1. *Set Clear Goals:*

Define your self-improvement objectives. Are you looking to learn a new skill, expand your knowledge, or gain insights into personal development? Having clear goals will help you stay focused.

2. *Effective Search Queries:*

Learn how to craft precise search queries to find relevant resources quickly. Utilize advanced search techniques like using quotation marks for exact phrases or employing specific keywords.

3. *Explore a Variety of Formats:*

Information comes in various formats, including articles, videos, podcasts, and interactive tutorials. Explore different formats to find the one that resonates with your learning style.

4. *Diversify Your Interests:*

While focusing on your primary self-improvement goals, don't hesitate to explore diverse topics. Serendipitous discoveries can lead to unexpected growth opportunities.

5. Regularly Check for Updates:

Google Bard frequently updates its algorithms and features. Stay informed about these changes to optimize your search experience and access new learning resources.

6. Engage with Experts:

Join forums, communities, or online courses related to your self-improvement journey. Engaging with experts and peers can provide valuable insights and support.

7. Time Management:

Effective time management is crucial for self-improvement. Allocate dedicated time for learning and ensure you maintain a healthy balance with other responsibilities.

8. Practice Critical Thinking:

While Google Bard provides a wealth of information, critical thinking is essential. Evaluate sources, cross-reference information, and develop your analytical skills.

9. Measure Progress:

Track your progress in your self-improvement journey. This could involve maintaining a journal, setting milestones, or using specialized apps and tools.

10. Experiment and Apply Knowledge:
Learning is most effective when you apply what you've l earned. Experiment with new skills, apply knowledge in real-life situations, and embrace a growth mindset.

In conclusion, Google Bard is a versatile tool that can empower you to embark on a journey of self-improvement and lifelong learning. By setting clear goals, utilizing effective search techniques, and staying open to diverse interests, you can leverage this platform to expand your horizons, acquire new skills, and foster personal growth. Whether you're pursuing professional development, exploring hobbies, or seeking personal enlightenment, Google Bard is your gateway to a world of knowledge and self-discovery.

15.2 Lifelong Learning and Skill Development

Lifelong learning is a fundamental concept in today's rapidly changing world. It encompasses the idea that learning is not limited to formal education but should be a continuous, self-driven process that extends throughout one's life. Google Bard plays a crucial role in facilitating lifelong learning by providing access to a wealth of information, resources, and opportunities for skill development. In this section, we will delve into the significance of lifelong learning, how Google Bard supports it, and practical strategies to enhance your skills.

The Importance of Lifelong Learning

1. Adaptation to Change:

The pace of technological advancements and societal changes requires individuals to adapt continuously. Lifelong learning equips you with the skills needed to navigate evolving landscapes effectively.

2. Professional Growth:

In the workplace, staying updated with the latest trends and acquiring new skills can enhance your career prospects and job security. Continuous learning is an investment in your professional growth.

3. Personal Fulfillment:

Learning new things can be personally fulfilling and lead to a sense of achievement and satisfaction. It broadens your horizons and enriches your life experiences.

4. Problem-Solving Abilities:

Lifelong learners tend to have better problem-solving skills. They can approach challenges with creativity and a growth mindset, leading to innovative solutions.

5. Remaining Relevant:

In a knowledge-based economy, staying relevant is crucial. Lifelong learning ensures that you remain up-to-date and competitive in various aspects of your life.

Google Bard as a Lifelong Learning Tool

Google Bard offers several features and resources that support lifelong learning and skill development:

1. Access to Vast Knowledge:

The internet is a treasure trove of information, and Google Bard helps you access it quickly. Whether you're looking for academic papers, how-to guides, or video tutorials, it's all at your fingertips.

2. Educational Platforms and Courses:

Google Bard can direct you to online learning platforms, such as Coursera, edX, Khan Academy, and many more. These platforms offer courses on a wide range of topics, allowing you to acquire new skills or deepen existing ones.

3. Book and Literature Search:

If you prefer learning from books, Google Bard can assist in finding relevant literature. It can provide information about books, their availability, and even offer previews.

4. Exploration of Diverse Interests:

Lifelong learning often involves exploring diverse interests. Google Bard's recommendations and search results can introduce you to new subjects and areas of knowledge.

5. Skill Acquisition:

Whether it's coding, cooking, photography, or any other skill, Google Bard can guide you with tutorials, forums, and resources to help you develop your abilities.

6. Stay Informed:

Keeping up with current events, news, and trends is part of lifelong learning. Google Bard provides access to the latest information, allowing you to stay informed and aware.

Strategies for Effective Lifelong Learning

To make the most of Google Bard as a tool for lifelong learning and skill development, consider the following strategies:

1. Set Clear Learning Goals:

Define what you want to learn and achieve. Having clear goals will guide your learning journey and keep you motivated.

2. Utilize Online Courses:

Enroll in online courses on platforms recommended by Google Bard. These courses often come with structured lessons and assessments.

3. Diversify Your Learning Sources:

Don't rely on a single source of information. Explore multiple perspectives, books, articles, and video content to gain a well-rounded understanding.

4. Practice Regularly:

Skill development requires consistent practice. Dedicate time each day or week to apply what you've learned.

5. Seek Feedback and Guidance:

Connect with experts, mentors, or online communities related to your field of interest. They can provide valuable feedback and guidance.

6. Reflect and Adapt:

Periodically review your progress, adapt your learning strategies, and refine your goals based on your experiences.

In conclusion, lifelong learning and skill development are essential for personal and professional growth. Google Bard serves as a powerful tool to facilitate this process by providing access to a world of knowledge and learning opportunities. By setting clear goals, utilizing online courses, diversifying your learning sources, and practicing regularly, you can harness the potential of Google Bard to enhance your skills and expand your horizons throughout your life.

15.3 Exploring Diverse Topics and Interests

Exploring diverse topics and interests is a hallmark of lifelong learning, and Google Bard is an invaluable tool for this endeavor. In this section, we will discuss the importance of exploring diverse subjects, how Google Bard can assist you in this journey, and practical tips to make the most of your explorations.

The Significance of Exploring Diverse Topics

1. Broadening Horizons:

Exploring diverse topics exposes you to different perspectives, cultures, and ideas, broadening your horizons and fostering open-mindedness.

2. Cross-Disciplinary Insights:

Many breakthroughs occur at the intersection of different fields. By delving into unrelated subjects, you may discover innovative solutions or gain unique insights in your area of expertise.

3. Enhanced Creativity:

Diverse knowledge fuels creativity. The more you know about various topics, the more creative connections you can make.

4. Personal Growth:

Learning about different subjects contributes to personal growth and self-discovery. It can help you identify new passions and interests.

5. Adaptability:

In a rapidly changing world, adaptability is a valuable trait. Being knowledgeable about various topics equips you with the ability to adapt to different situations and challenges.

Leveraging Google Bard for Diverse Exploration

Google Bard offers several features that can facilitate your exploration of diverse topics and interests:

1. Recommended Content:

Google Bard's recommendation algorithms suggest articles, videos, and websites based on your search history and interests. These recommendations can introduce you to new subjects.

2. News and Trends:

Stay updated with the latest news and trends in various fields. Google Bard provides access to news articles and trending topics, allowing you to explore what's happening around the world.

3. Book Recommendations:

If you're interested in reading, Google Bard can recommend books related to your searches. You can discover books on diverse subjects and explore them further.

4. Exploration Queries:

Use Google Bard to ask open-ended questions like "What are the emerging technologies in healthcare?" or "Tell me about lesser-known historical events." Such queries can lead you to fascinating discoveries.

5. Follow Your Curiosity:

Don't hesitate to follow your curiosity. If a topic piques your interest, explore it further by clicking on relevant search results and diving deeper into the content.

Tips for Effective Exploration

To make your exploration of diverse topics and interests more effective, consider these tips:

1. Maintain an Open Mind:

Approach new subjects with an open and curious mind. Embrace the opportunity to learn something new.

2. Set Aside Time for Exploration:

Dedicate specific time slots in your schedule for exploring diverse topics. Consistency is key to broadening your knowledge.

3. Take Notes and Reflect:

Keep a journal of your explorations. Write down what you've learned and how it connects to your existing knowledge.

4. Engage in Discussions:

Join online forums, discussion groups, or social media communities related to the topics you're exploring. Engaging in discussions can deepen your understanding.

5. Share Your Discoveries:

Share interesting articles, insights, or discoveries with your friends and peers. Sharing knowledge can spark meaningful conversations.

6. Stay Updated:

Keep up with the latest developments in the fields you're exploring. Subscribe to newsletters, follow experts on social media, and read industry publications.

In conclusion, exploring diverse topics and interests is a rewarding aspect of lifelong learning. It broadens your perspective, enhances creativity, and contributes to personal growth. Google Bard, with its wealth of information and recommendation features, serves as an excellent companion on your journey of exploration. By maintaining an open mind, setting aside time for exploration, taking notes, engaging in discussions, sharing your discoveries, and staying updated, you can make the most of Google Bard to expand your knowledge in diverse directions.

15.4 Staying Informed and Curious

Staying informed and curious is an essential mindset for continuous learning and personal development. In this section, we'll explore the importance of curiosity, how to nurture it, and how Google Bard can be a valuable tool in your quest for knowledge.

The Significance of Curiosity

Curiosity is a driving force behind human progress. It's the desire to understand, question, and explore the unknown. Here are some reasons why curiosity is crucial:

1. Fuels Lifelong Learning:

Curiosity fuels the desire to learn. When you're curious, you actively seek out information and experiences, leading to continuous growth.

2. Problem-Solving:

Curious individuals are often better problem-solvers because they seek creative solutions and approaches.

3. Adaptability:

Curiosity fosters adaptability, a valuable skill in today's fast-changing world. You're more open to change and new ideas.

4. Inspiration:

Curiosity can lead to inspiration. Discovering new things can spark creativity and innovative thinking.

5. Personal Fulfillment:

Learning and exploring can be deeply fulfilling. Curiosity adds meaning to life by making it a journey of discovery.

Nurturing Curiosity

Here are strategies to nurture and maintain your curiosity:

1. Ask Questions:

Cultivate a habit of asking questions about the world around you. No question is too small or insignificant.

2. Read Widely:

Explore diverse subjects through books, articles, and online resources. Don't limit yourself to your comfort zone.

3. Experiment and Explore:

Try new activities, visit new places, or experiment with hobbies. Novel experiences often pique curiosity.

4. Connect with Experts:

Engage with experts and enthusiasts in fields that interest you. Conversations with knowledgeable individuals can be inspiring.

5. Stay Curious About Curiosity:

Reflect on what makes you curious and why. Understanding your own curiosity can help you nurture it better.

Google Bard as a Curiosity Companion

Google Bard can be a powerful ally in your pursuit of curiosity. Here's how to leverage it effectively:

1. Search Queries:

Craft specific search queries based on your interests or questions. Google Bard's search capabilities can quickly provide information on a wide range of topics.

2. Follow Trends:

Use Google Bard to stay updated on current trends, news, and developments in your areas of curiosity.

3. Read Reviews and Recommendations:

Before diving into a new book, movie, or restaurant, use Google Bard to read reviews and recommendations from experts and fellow enthusiasts.

4. Discover New Content:

Google Bard can suggest related articles, videos, and websites based on your searches. This feature can lead you to unexpected discoveries.

5. Access Learning Resources:

Explore online courses, tutorials, and educational materials related to your curious interests. Google Bard can direct you to reputable sources.

Practical Tips for Staying Curious

To stay curious effectively, consider these practical tips:

1. Set Learning Goals:

Define what you want to learn or explore next. Having clear goals can motivate your curiosity.

2. Join Communities:

Join online communities, forums, or social media groups dedicated to your interests. Engaging with like-minded individuals can keep your curiosity alive.

3. Take Breaks:

Don't forget to take breaks and recharge. A fresh perspective can reignite your curiosity.

4. Share Knowledge:

Share interesting findings or insights with others. Teaching or discussing what you've learned can reinforce your own understanding and curiosity.

5. Embrace Failure:

Curiosity involves taking risks and sometimes failing. Embrace failures as learning experiences that fuel your curiosity.

In conclusion, staying informed and curious is a lifelong journey. Curiosity is a powerful driver of learning, problem-solving, and personal growth. By nurturing your curiosity through asking questions, reading widely, experimenting, connecting with experts, and staying curious about curiosity itself, you can embark on a fulfilling journey of discovery. Google Bard, with its vast resources and search capabilities, can be your trusty companion in this quest for knowledge and curiosity. So, embrace your innate curiosity, keep asking questions, and let your thirst for understanding guide you to new horizons.

15.5 Balancing Technology with Personal Growth

In the age of digital technology and AI-powered search engines like Google Bard, it's crucial to strike a balance between leveraging these tools for personal development and nurturing other aspects of personal growth. While technology offers unparalleled access to information and resources, it can also be a double-edged sword that, if not managed mindfully, may hinder holistic development.

The Digital Age Dilemma

As we navigate the digital age, we encounter several challenges related to technology and personal growth:

1. Information Overload:

The abundance of information available online can lead to information overload, making it challenging to filter and prioritize knowledge.

2. Dependency on Technology:

Relying excessively on technology can diminish critical thinking skills, problem-solving abilities, and self-reliance.

3. Reduced Face-to-Face Interaction:

Increased screen time can lead to decreased face-to-face social interaction, potentially affecting communication and interpersonal skills.

4. Distraction and Multitasking:

Constant connectivity can encourage multitasking and distractions, hindering deep focus and productivity.

5. Privacy and Security Concerns:

Sharing personal information online can pose privacy and security risks, necessitating caution and awareness.

Strategies for Balancing Technology and Personal Growth

Achieving a balance between technology and personal growth requires deliberate strategies:

1. Digital Detox:

Periodically disconnect from digital devices to recharge, reflect, and engage in offline activities that promote personal well-being.

2. Set Boundaries:

Establish boundaries for screen time, especially during personal and family time, to maintain a healthy balance.

3. Embrace Mindfulness:

Practice mindfulness techniques to stay present, reduce stress, and enhance self-awareness amid digital distractions.

4. Diversify Learning Sources:

While technology offers vast learning resources, explore traditional learning methods such as books, workshops, and hands-on experiences.

5. Critical Thinking:

Cultivate critical thinking skills by evaluating information critically, discerning credible sources, and questioning assumptions.

6. Physical Well-Being:

Prioritize physical health through regular exercise, balanced nutrition, and adequate sleep, recognizing that these factors influence personal growth.

7. Social Interaction:

Nurture meaningful face-to-face relationships and engage in community activities to develop social and emotional intelligence.

8. Life-Long Learning:

Embrace the concept of lifelong learning by continuously seeking knowledge beyond digital resources, fostering curiosity and adaptability.

Google Bard as an Ally in Balance

Google Bard can play a role in maintaining balance by providing targeted and efficient access to information. Here's how to utilize it effectively:

1. Set Intentions:

Before searching, clarify your intentions and desired outcomes to avoid aimless browsing.

2. Utilize Filters:

Use search filters and advanced options to refine results and find information more efficiently.

3. Scheduled Learning:

Dedicate specific time slots for learning through Google Bard, ensuring it doesn't encroach upon other aspects of personal growth.

4. Engage Mindfully:

When using Google Bard, practice focused attention and mindful searching rather than succumbing to distractions.

5. Privacy Awareness:

Be conscious of privacy settings and data security while using online search engines and platforms.

Conclusion

Balancing technology with personal growth is an ongoing endeavor that requires conscious choices and mindfulness. While technology like Google Bard is a valuable tool for learning and information access, it's essential to use it mindfully and ensure it enhances, rather than hinders, your holistic personal development. By setting boundaries, embracing offline experiences, nurturing critical thinking, and prioritizing well-being, you can harness the benefits of technology while nurturing your overall growth and well-being. Striking this balance empowers you to thrive in the digital age while remaining grounded in your personal journey of development and self-discovery.

Chapter 16: Google Bard in Creative Industries

Section 16.1: Assisting Writers and Journalists

In today's fast-paced world, where information is continuously being generated and disseminated, writers and journalists often find themselves in need of efficient tools to aid their research and content creation processes. Google Bard, with its powerful AI-driven capabilities, has become an invaluable companion for professionals in the creative industries, including writers and journalists.

Enhancing Research Efforts

Writers and journalists frequently require extensive research to gather accurate information and insights for their articles and reports. Google Bard's advanced search techniques and access to a vast array of data sources make it an ideal tool for conducting research. By crafting precise search queries, users can uncover relevant articles, academic papers, and news reports with ease. Additionally, the ability to filter search results based on publication date ensures that writers and journalists can access the most up-to-date information.

Improving Writing Efficiency

Writing is a complex process that often involves juggling multiple tasks simultaneously. Google Bard simplifies this process by offering features such as voice-to-text transcription, which allows writers to dictate their thoughts and have them converted into text. This not only accelerates the writing process but also reduces the risk of writer's block. Furthermore, the AI-powered grammar and style suggestions provided by Google Bard can help improve the quality of written content, ensuring it meets professional standards.

Tracking Trends and Events

For journalists, staying informed about current events and emerging trends is crucial. Google Bard's integration with news sources and real-time updates enables journalists to track breaking news and trending topics effortlessly. By setting up custom alerts and monitoring specific keywords, journalists can receive notifications about developments in their areas of interest, enabling them to cover stories as they unfold.

Collaborative Research and Data Sharing

Collaboration is often a key aspect of content creation in the creative industries. Google Bard facilitates collaboration by allowing users to share search results, articles, and research findings with colleagues and collaborators seamlessly. This collaborative environment encourages the exchange of ideas and insights, fostering a more productive and efficient workflow.

Ethical Considerations

While Google Bard offers numerous benefits to writers and journalists, it is essential to consider the ethical implications of using AI-powered tools in the creative process. Journalists, in particular, must uphold principles of accuracy, fairness, and transparency in their reporting. As such, it is crucial to use AI tools like Google Bard responsibly and ensure that the information gathered is verified from credible sources.

In summary, Google Bard has emerged as a valuable asset for writers and journalists, streamlining research, improving writing efficiency, and facilitating collaboration. However, users must remain mindful of ethical considerations to maintain the integrity of their work in the creative industries.

Section 16.2: Supporting Artists and Designers

Artists and designers often rely on inspiration, reference materials, and creative tools to bring their visions to life. Google Bard plays a significant role in supporting and enhancing the creative process for individuals in these fields. Whether it's finding inspiration, accessing reference materials, or using AI-driven design tools, Google Bard has become an indispensable companion for artists and designers.

Finding Visual Inspiration

One of the primary challenges artists and designers face is finding visual inspiration for their projects. Google Bard simplifies this process by allowing users to perform image searches based on keywords, themes, or styles. Artists can explore a vast collection of images, artwork, and photographs from various sources, helping them discover new ideas and concepts for their work.

Accessing Reference Materials

Reference materials are essential for artists and designers seeking to create realistic and accurate artwork. Google Bard provides easy access to reference materials such as photographs, illustrations, and diagrams. Whether an artist is looking for anatomical references for figure drawing or architectural blueprints for a design project, Google Bard's extensive database offers a wealth of resources.

AI-Powered Design Tools

Google Bard's AI-driven capabilities extend to design and creative tasks. Artists and designers can leverage AI-powered tools for tasks like image enhancement, color palette generation, and even design suggestions. For instance, AI algorithms can help identify complementary color schemes or suggest layout improvements based on design principles. These tools not only save time but also enhance the overall quality of the creative work.

Researching Art Movements and Styles

Artists often draw inspiration from historical art movements and styles. Google Bard's advanced search capabilities enable users to delve into the history of art and explore various movements, artists, and styles. By studying the works of renowned artists and understanding the context of different periods, artists can enrich their artistic knowledge and incorporate elements into their own creations.

Collaboration and Feedback

Collaboration among artists and designers is essential for creative growth and development. Google Bard supports collaboration by enabling users to share reference materials, artwork, and design concepts with colleagues and peers. Additionally, artists can seek feedback and critique from a global community of artists and designers, allowing them to refine their work and gain valuable insights.

Ethical Considerations

While Google Bard offers substantial benefits to artists and designers, ethical considerations must be taken into account. Artists should respect copyright and intellectual property rights when using reference materials and images found online. Additionally, the use of AI-driven design tools should be balanced with the artist's unique creative expression, ensuring that the human touch remains central to the artistic process.

In conclusion, Google Bard serves as a valuable resource for artists and designers, offering visual inspiration, access to reference materials, AI-powered design tools, and opportunities for collaboration. When used responsibly and ethically, Google Bard can enhance the creative process and empower individuals in these creative fields to achieve their artistic visions.

Section 16.3: Enhancing Music and Entertainment Research

Google Bard has made significant contributions to the fields of music and entertainment by providing researchers and enthusiasts with powerful tools and resources for exploration, analysis, and creativity. This section explores how individuals involved in music and entertainment benefit from the capabilities offered by Google Bard.

Exploring Music and Entertainment History

Researchers and music historians can rely on Google Bard to explore the rich history of music and entertainment. The search engine's vast database includes archives of music recordings, interviews, documentaries, and historical documents related to music and entertainment figures and events. Whether studying the evolution of music genres or tracing the careers of iconic artists, Google Bard offers access to a wealth of information.

Music Theory and Composition

Composers and music enthusiasts can use Google Bard to dive into music theory, composition techniques, and musical analysis. Search queries can yield results ranging from sheet music and instructional resources to scholarly articles and analyses of musical works. This wealth of information aids composers in refining their craft, exploring new musical ideas, and understanding the intricacies of different music styles and genres.

Access to Performances and Concerts

Google Bard facilitates access to recorded music performances and concert footage, providing a valuable resource for music educators, performers, and enthusiasts. Users can find recordings of live concerts, recitals, and masterclasses across various genres and time periods. This access enables musicians to study performances by renowned artists, gain insights into interpretation, and learn from live musical experiences.

Discovering New Artists and Music

Music enthusiasts are constantly seeking fresh and exciting music to listen to. Google Bard's recommendation algorithms, in combination with user-generated content and reviews, help users discover new artists, albums, and songs. Whether exploring emerging indie bands or diving into niche musical subcultures, users can curate their music libraries and broaden their musical horizons.

Analyzing Trends and Pop Culture

Researchers and entertainment analysts can utilize Google Bard to monitor trends and developments within the music and entertainment industries. By examining search trends, news articles, and social media discussions, analysts can gain insights into audience preferences, emerging trends, and the impact of cultural phenomena. This information is invaluable for making informed decisions in marketing, programming, and content creation.

Ethical Considerations

While Google Bard offers vast resources for music and entertainment research, ethical considerations must be taken into account. Respect for copyright and intellectual property rights is paramount when using audiovisual content found online. Users should be aware of licensing agreements and permissions when using music and entertainment materials for educational, research, or creative purposes.

In summary, Google Bard empowers individuals in the music and entertainment fields by providing access to historical records, music theory resources, performances, new music discoveries, and trend analysis. When used responsibly and ethically, Google Bard serves as a versatile tool for enhancing research, creativity, and understanding within these vibrant and dynamic domains.

Section 16.4: AI's Role in Creative Inspiration

Artists and creators across various disciplines have found inspiration and support in Google Bard, thanks to its AI-powered capabilities. This section explores how AI contributes to creative inspiration and the development of artistic projects.

Creative Content Generation

Google Bard offers tools and resources that assist artists and writers in generating creative content. AI-powered writing assistance tools can provide suggestions, expand ideas, and offer alternative phrasing, helping writers overcome creative blocks and enhance their writing style. Visual artists can also benefit from AI-driven art generators that offer design ideas, color palettes, and artistic concepts.

Music Composition and Arrangement

Musicians and composers can use AI algorithms integrated into Google Bard to aid in music composition and arrangement. AI-powered software can generate musical compositions, suggest harmonies, and even create orchestral arrangements based on user input. This not only speeds up the creative process but also introduces novel musical ideas that artists can explore and adapt.

Visual Arts and Design

Visual artists, graphic designers, and illustrators can leverage AI for artistic inspiration and assistance. AI algorithms can analyze existing artwork, providing insights into artistic styles, techniques, and composition. Artists can explore different design elements and experiment with various artistic approaches by using AI as a source of inspiration.

Interactive Storytelling

AI-driven interactive storytelling platforms can be used to create immersive narratives and digital experiences. Writers and game developers can employ AI to dynamically adapt storylines, characters, and outcomes based on user interactions. This allows for personalized storytelling experiences that engage audiences in unique and unexpected ways.

Cross-Disciplinary Collaboration

Google Bard promotes cross-disciplinary collaboration by connecting artists, writers, musicians, and designers from different backgrounds. Collaborative projects that combine various artistic mediums are increasingly common, with artists using AI to bridge the gaps between disciplines and explore new creative horizons.

Ethical Considerations

While AI can be a powerful tool for creative inspiration, ethical considerations should be taken into account. Artists and creators should be mindful of the responsible use of AI-generated content, giving proper credit and adhering to copyright and intellectual property regulations. Additionally, creators should strike a balance between AI assistance and their unique artistic voice, ensuring that AI complements their creative process rather than overshadowing it.

In conclusion, Google Bard's AI-powered features have become a valuable resource for artists and creators seeking inspiration and assistance in their creative endeavors. Whether in writing, music composition, visual arts, interactive storytelling, or collaborative projects, AI plays a significant role in expanding the possibilities of artistic expression and innovation. As technology continues to evolve, the synergy between AI and creativity will likely yield even more exciting opportunities for artists and creators worldwide.

Section 16.5: Addressing Intellectual Property Concerns

The integration of AI into creative industries through platforms like Google Bard raises significant intellectual property (IP) concerns. Creators and rights holders must navigate these challenges to protect their work and ensure fair compensation. This section discusses the IP considerations associated with AI-driven creative content and explores potential solutions.

Ownership of AI-Generated Content

One of the primary concerns is determining the ownership of content generated or assisted by AI tools. In most cases, the person who initiates the AI process is considered the author or creator of the content. However, AI's role in content creation blurs traditional lines, leading to debates over authorship and ownership.

To address this issue, creators should carefully review the terms of service and licensing agreements of AI platforms like Google Bard. Some platforms may claim ownership or usage rights over AI-generated content, while others may grant creators full ownership. It's essential to understand these terms to protect your rights.

Copyright and AI-Generated Art

AI-generated art can pose unique challenges in the realm of copyright law. Copyright law typically protects original works created by humans. When AI is involved in art generation, determining whether it qualifies for copyright protection can be complex.

Creators should consult legal experts to understand the copyright implications of their AI-generated works. Some countries are adapting copyright laws to include AI-generated content, while others may require human involvement in the creative process for copyright protection to apply.

Attribution and Plagiarism

Proper attribution is critical when using AI-generated content, especially if it draws from existing copyrighted material. Creators should ensure that AI-generated text, images, or music comply with copyright laws and provide appropriate attribution when necessary. Failure to do so could lead to accusations of plagiarism or copyright infringement.

Licensing and Usage Agreements

Creators and organizations using AI-generated content should establish clear licensing and usage agreements. These agreements define how the content can be used, who owns it, and under what conditions it can be shared or sold. Licensing agreements can protect both creators and users of AI-generated content by outlining rights and responsibilities.

Monitoring and Enforcement

Monitoring and enforcing IP rights in the age of AI require vigilance. Creators should employ technologies and services that help identify unauthorized use of their content. AI-powered tools can assist in monitoring and detecting instances of content misuse, making it easier to take appropriate legal action when necessary.

Ethical Considerations

Beyond legal concerns, there are ethical considerations associated with AI-generated content. Creators should be transparent about the role of AI in their work and respect ethical guidelines regarding responsible AI usage. Fostering a culture of ethical creativity ensures that AI-driven art and content benefit both creators and society as a whole.

In conclusion, addressing intellectual property concerns in the context of AI-driven creative content is crucial for creators, artists, and organizations. By understanding ownership, copyright, attribution, licensing, monitoring, and ethical considerations, creators can harness the potential of AI while protecting their rights and contributing to a responsible and innovative creative landscape. As AI continues to evolve, staying informed about the latest legal and ethical developments is essential for anyone involved in AI-driven creative processes.

Chapter 17: Google Bard for Health and Wellness

Section 17.1: Accessing Health Information

Google Bard plays a significant role in providing access to health-related information, which can empower individuals to make informed decisions about their well-being. From understanding symptoms to researching treatment options, people turn to AI-powered search engines like Google Bard for health-related queries. This section delves into the importance of accessing health information online and how Google Bard can assist in this context.

The Importance of Accessible Health Information

In today's digital age, the internet has become a primary source of health information for many. People use search engines like Google Bard to seek answers to their health questions, learn about medical conditions, and explore potential treatments. Accessible health information is essential for several reasons:

1. **Empowering Patients:** Access to accurate and reliable health information empowers individuals to take an active role in their healthcare decisions. Informed patients are better equipped to discuss their concerns with healthcare professionals and participate in treatment choices.

2. **Raising Health Awareness:** Health information online can raise awareness about various medical conditions,

preventive measures, and lifestyle choices. This can lead to healthier behaviors and improved public health outcomes.

3. **Remote Health Management:** Online health information enables individuals to manage certain health conditions remotely. Patients can monitor their symptoms, follow treatment guidelines, and seek virtual consultations when needed.

4. **Supporting Caregivers:** Caregivers, whether family members or healthcare professionals, benefit from access to up-to-date health information. It helps them provide better care and support to individuals with medical needs.

5. **Reducing Stigma:** Accessible health information can reduce the stigma associated with certain medical conditions. By increasing understanding and empathy, it promotes a more inclusive and compassionate society.

Google Bard's Role in Health Information Access

Google Bard plays a crucial role in facilitating access to health information for users around the world. Its AI-powered search capabilities enable users to find relevant and trustworthy health content quickly. Here's how Google Bard supports health and wellness:

1. **Accurate Search Results:** Google Bard's algorithms prioritize reputable sources of health information, ensuring that users receive accurate and up-to-date results for their health queries.

2. **Symptom Identification:** Users can input symptoms into Google Bard's search bar, which may provide them with information about potential medical conditions. However, it's important to note that Google Bard's symptom checker is not a substitute for professional medical advice.

3. **Health Condition Information:** Google Bard provides detailed information about various medical conditions, including symptoms, causes, risk factors, diagnosis, and treatment options. Users can access summaries and links to authoritative sources.

4. **Local Health Resources:** Google Bard can also assist users in finding nearby healthcare providers, pharmacies, hospitals, and clinics. This feature is particularly useful when seeking immediate medical attention.

5. **Wellness and Prevention:** Beyond addressing medical conditions, Google Bard offers information on general wellness, preventive measures, and healthy lifestyle choices. Users can explore topics like nutrition, fitness, mental health, and more.

6. **Medical News and Updates:** Google Bard aggregates the latest medical news and research findings, keeping users informed about breakthroughs in the field of healthcare.

Caution and Responsible Use

While Google Bard provides valuable health information, users should exercise caution and use the platform responsibly. It's important to remember the following:

- **Consult Healthcare Professionals:** For specific medical concerns or conditions, it's essential to consult healthcare professionals who can provide personalized guidance and treatment plans.

- **Verify Information:** Always verify health information from multiple reputable sources. Consult medical journals, government health agencies, and healthcare organizations for the most accurate and reliable information.

- **Avoid Self-Diagnosis:** While Google Bard can provide information about symptoms and conditions, it should not be used for self-diagnosis. Always seek professional medical evaluation and diagnosis.

- **Privacy Considerations:** Users should be aware of the privacy implications when searching for health information online. Personal health data should be handled with care and protected according to relevant regulations.

In conclusion, Google Bard's role in providing access to health information is invaluable in today's digital age. It empowers individuals to become more informed and proactive about their health and wellness. However, users should approach health-related queries with caution, seek professional medical advice when needed, and verify information from reliable sources to make informed decisions about their health.

Section 17.2: Evaluating Medical Research and Data

In the age of digital information, the availability of medical research and data on the internet has grown exponentially. This wealth of information empowers individuals, healthcare professionals, and researchers to access the latest studies, clinical trials, and health data. Section 17.2 explores the importance of evaluating medical research and data online and provides guidance on how to navigate this vast landscape effectively.

The Significance of Medical Research and Data

Medical research and data are foundational to advancements in healthcare. They drive innovations in treatments, pharmaceuticals, medical devices, and our understanding of various diseases and conditions. Access to credible and up-to-date research is crucial for several reasons:

1. **Informed Decision-Making:** Healthcare professionals rely on medical research to make evidence-based decisions about patient care, treatment options, and interventions.

2. **Patient Empowerment:** Patients and caregivers can benefit from understanding the latest research findings, enabling them to actively participate in healthcare discussions and make informed choices.

3. **Advancing Medicine:** Researchers use medical data and studies to develop new therapies, diagnostics, and preventive measures. Accessible research accelerates medical progress.

4. **Global Health:** Medical research informs public health policies, disease surveillance, and responses to global health crises such as pandemics. It plays a vital role in safeguarding public health.

5. **Education and Training:** Medical students, professionals, and scientists rely on research publications to expand their knowledge and expertise in their respective fields.

Evaluating Medical Research Online

As medical research becomes increasingly available online, it's essential to develop skills for evaluating the credibility and relevance of the information you encounter. Here are some key considerations when evaluating medical research and data on the internet:

1. **Source Credibility:** Begin by assessing the source of the research. Is it published in a reputable medical journal or from a recognized healthcare institution or university? Peer-reviewed journals are typically more reliable sources.

2. **Publication Date:** Check the publication date to ensure that the research is current and up-to-date. Medical knowledge evolves, and older studies may not reflect the latest findings.

3. **Study Design:** Understand the research methodology used in the study. Was it a randomized controlled trial, a cohort study, or another type of research design? The study design affects the reliability of the findings.

4. **Sample Size:** Consider the sample size of the study. Larger sample sizes generally provide more reliable results. Small studies may have limited statistical power.

5. **Conflicts of Interest:** Look for potential conflicts of interest. Did the researchers receive funding from pharmaceutical companies or other organizations that could bias the results?

6. **Peer Review:** Peer-reviewed research has been evaluated by experts in the field for quality and validity. It's generally more trustworthy than non-peer-reviewed sources.

7. **Consistency with Established Knowledge:** Check if the research aligns with established medical knowledge and guidelines. It should contribute to the existing body of evidence rather than contradict it.

8. **Methodology Transparency:** Transparent reporting of methods and results is crucial. Ensure that the study provides sufficient detail for others to replicate the research.

9. **Discussion of Limitations:** Reliable research acknowledges its limitations. Be cautious of studies that make grandiose claims without discussing potential shortcomings.

Accessing Medical Research Databases

To access high-quality medical research and data, consider using reputable medical research databases and academic search engines. Some popular options include:

- **PubMed:** A free database of biomedical literature that includes a vast collection of medical research articles.

- **Google Scholar:** A search engine for scholarly articles, including medical research, offering a wide range of sources.

- **ScienceDirect:** A platform that provides access to scientific, technical, and medical research articles.

- **JSTOR:** An extensive digital library that offers access to academic journals, books, and primary source materials.

- **Web of Science:** A multidisciplinary research database that covers a wide range of scientific disciplines, including medicine.

The Role of AI in Medical Research

Artificial intelligence (AI) is increasingly being utilized in medical research and data analysis. AI algorithms can analyze large datasets, identify patterns, and assist in drug discovery, disease diagnosis, and treatment optimization. Researchers and healthcare professionals can leverage AI-powered tools to streamline their work and access insights that were previously challenging to obtain.

In conclusion, the internet provides a wealth of medical research and data that can benefit individuals, healthcare providers, and researchers. However, it's crucial to approach online medical information critically and evaluate the credibility and relevance of the sources. By honing your skills in assessing research quality and using reputable databases, you can harness the power of medical research to make informed healthcare decisions and contribute to advancements in the field.

Section 17.3: Wellness Tips and Resources

Wellness is a holistic concept that encompasses physical, mental, and emotional well-being. In Section 17.3, we delve into wellness tips and resources to help you maintain and improve your overall health. Achieving and maintaining wellness is a lifelong journey, and it involves making informed choices and adopting healthy habits.

Understanding Wellness

Wellness is not merely the absence of illness but a proactive approach to living a healthier and more fulfilling life. It involves taking steps to prevent health issues, manage stress, nurture relationships, and find balance in various aspects of life. Here are some key components of wellness:

1. **Physical Wellness:** This involves taking care of your body through regular exercise, a balanced diet, adequate sleep, and preventive healthcare measures. Physical wellness contributes to overall vitality and energy.

2. **Mental Wellness:** Mental wellness encompasses emotional and psychological well-being. It involves managing stress, practicing mindfulness, seeking support when needed, and maintaining a positive outlook on life.

3. **Emotional Wellness:** Emotional wellness involves recognizing and managing your emotions effectively. It includes developing healthy coping mechanisms and fostering resilience in the face of life's challenges.

4. **Social Wellness:** Social connections and relationships are essential for well-being. Cultivating healthy relationships, fostering a sense of belonging, and

maintaining a supportive social network contribute to social wellness.

5. **Intellectual Wellness:** Intellectual wellness involves lifelong learning and personal growth. It includes engaging in stimulating activities, pursuing interests and hobbies, and expanding your knowledge.

6. **Occupational Wellness:** Occupational wellness relates to satisfaction and fulfillment in your work or chosen occupation. It involves finding meaning and purpose in your professional life.

7. **Spiritual Wellness:** Spiritual wellness is about exploring your values, beliefs, and purpose in life. It may involve practices like meditation, prayer, or connecting with nature.

Wellness Tips

Maintaining wellness requires intentional effort and the adoption of healthy habits. Here are some wellness tips to consider:

1. **Stay Active:** Incorporate regular physical activity into your routine. Whether it's walking, jogging, yoga, or dancing, find activities you enjoy to stay active.

2. **Eat Nutritious Foods:** Consume a balanced diet rich in fruits, vegetables, whole grains, lean proteins, and healthy fats. Stay hydrated by drinking plenty of water.

3. **Prioritize Sleep:** Aim for 7-9 hours of quality sleep each night. A good night's sleep is essential for physical and mental well-being.

4. **Manage Stress:** Practice stress management techniques such as deep breathing, meditation, or progressive muscle relaxation to reduce stress levels.

5. **Connect Socially:** Foster meaningful relationships with family and friends. Spending time with loved ones and maintaining a support system is vital for emotional wellness.

6. **Set Goals:** Establish clear goals and objectives for different aspects of your life. Having goals provides motivation and a sense of purpose.

7. **Practice Mindfulness:** Engage in mindfulness and meditation practices to enhance self-awareness and emotional regulation.

8. **Seek Professional Help:** If you're struggling with mental health issues or emotional challenges, don't hesitate to seek support from a mental health professional.

9. **Learn Continuously:** Feed your intellectual wellness by reading, exploring new interests, and participating in lifelong learning activities.

10. **Stay Organized:** Maintain a well-organized and clutter-free environment to reduce stress and improve productivity.

11. **Practice Gratitude:** Reflect on the things you're grateful for. Practicing gratitude can enhance your overall outlook on life.

12. **Stay Informed:** Stay up-to-date with healthcare recommendations and preventive measures to protect your physical health.

Wellness Resources

Numerous resources are available to support your wellness journey. Here are some sources to explore:

1. **Healthcare Providers:** Consult with healthcare professionals for personalized guidance on your physical and mental health.

2. **Wellness Apps:** There are various wellness apps that offer guidance on fitness, meditation, nutrition, and mental well-being.

3. **Online Communities:** Join online wellness communities or forums where you can connect with others on similar wellness journeys.

4. **Books and Publications:** Read books, articles, and publications related to wellness, self-help, and personal development.

5. **Local Programs:** Look for local wellness programs, workshops, and classes that offer opportunities for personal growth and improvement.

6. **Mental Health Services:** If you're struggling with mental health issues, consider seeking help from therapists, counselors, or support groups.

7. **Nutritionists and Dietitians:** Consult with nutrition experts to create a personalized diet plan that aligns with your wellness goals.

8. **Fitness Centers:** Explore fitness centers, gyms, or yoga studios in your area to find exercise programs that suit your preferences.

9. **Mindfulness and Meditation Resources:** Many resources, including apps and online courses, can guide you in practicing mindfulness and meditation.

10. **Health Websites:** Trustworthy websites and organizations provide information on various aspects of wellness, including nutrition, fitness, and

Section 17.4: Navigating Health-Related Queries Responsibly

In an era where information is readily available at our fingertips, it's common for individuals to turn to the internet for health-related information and advice. Section 17.4 discusses the importance of navigating health-related queries responsibly, understanding the risks involved, and making informed decisions when seeking health information online.

The Prevalence of Online Health Information

The internet has transformed the way people access health information. Websites, forums, social media, and search engines provide a plethora of health-related content. While this accessibility can be empowering, it also presents challenges, including misinformation, outdated information, and biased sources.

The Benefits of Online Health Information

1. **Empowerment:** Access to health information allows individuals to become more proactive in managing their health and making informed decisions about treatment options.

2. **Convenience:** Online resources provide quick access to a wide range of health information, which can be especially valuable when seeking information about common health issues and symptoms.

3. **Support and Community:** Online communities and forums enable individuals with similar health concerns to connect, share experiences, and offer support.

The Risks of Online Health Information

1. **Misinformation:** Not all online health information is accurate or reliable. Misinformation and myths can be easily disseminated, leading to misconceptions and potentially harmful decisions.

2. **Overdiagnosis and Anxiety:** Access to extensive health information can sometimes lead to overdiagnosis and unnecessary anxiety. People may misinterpret normal variations in health as serious conditions.

3. **Privacy Concerns:** Sharing personal health information online can have privacy implications. Users should be cautious when participating in health-related discussions on public forums.

Responsible Navigation of Online Health Information

To navigate health-related queries responsibly, consider the following guidelines:

1. **Verify Sources:** Rely on reputable sources such as government health agencies, medical institutions, and peer-reviewed journals. Check the publication date of the information to ensure its relevance.

2. **Consult Healthcare Professionals:** While online information can be valuable, consult healthcare professionals for personalized advice and treatment recommendations.

3. **Avoid Self-Diagnosis:** Avoid making self-diagnoses based solely on online information. Symptoms can be associated with various conditions, and a healthcare provider's expertise is essential for accurate diagnosis.

4. **Evaluate Credibility:** Assess the credibility of websites and sources. Look for evidence-based information and be cautious of sites promoting unproven treatments or miracle cures.

5. **Use Multiple Sources:** Cross-reference information from multiple reputable sources to ensure accuracy and reliability.

6. **Beware of Personal Bias:** Acknowledge that personal biases and anecdotes may influence online discussions.

Consider a balanced perspective and consult professionals for objective guidance.

7. **Protect Personal Information:** Be cautious about sharing personal health information on public forums or with unverified sources. Protect your privacy and confidentiality.

8. **Ask Questions:** Don't hesitate to ask questions and seek clarification when engaging in online health discussions. Encourage evidence-based answers.

9. **Stay Informed:** Continue learning about health-related topics, but do so responsibly. Understand the limitations of your own knowledge and seek professional guidance when needed.

10. **Seek Support:** If you're dealing with a health issue, consider joining online communities or support groups moderated by healthcare professionals or reputable organizations.

The Role of AI in Health Information

Artificial intelligence and machine learning are increasingly being used in healthcare to assist in diagnosing conditions, analyzing medical data, and providing health information. AI-powered chatbots and virtual assistants can offer guidance, but they should not replace consultation with healthcare professionals.

In summary, the internet offers a wealth of health-related information, but responsible navigation is crucial. By verifying sources, consulting healthcare professionals, and being discerning consumers of online health information, individuals can make more informed decisions about their well-being while minimizing the risks associated with misinformation and self-diagnosis.

Section 17.5: The Future of AI in Personal Health Management

As we advance further into the digital age, the role of artificial intelligence (AI) in personal health management is poised for significant growth. Section 17.5 explores the potential and challenges of AI in reshaping how individuals monitor, assess, and improve their health.

The Current Landscape

AI is already making inroads into personal health management through wearable devices, mobile apps, and smart health technologies. These technologies collect data on various health parameters, such as heart rate, sleep patterns, activity levels, and even emotional states. AI algorithms then analyze this data to provide insights, suggestions, and early warnings about potential health issues.

Key Applications of AI in Personal Health

1. **Personalized Health Insights:** AI can analyze vast amounts of health data to provide personalized recommendations for nutrition, exercise, and sleep, helping individuals make lifestyle changes that align with their specific needs and goals.

2. **Chronic Disease Management:** AI-powered tools can assist individuals with chronic conditions, such as diabetes or hypertension, by monitoring vital signs, offering medication reminders, and providing real-time feedback to both patients and healthcare providers.

3. **Mental Health Support:** AI-driven chatbots and virtual therapists are becoming more sophisticated in providing emotional support, identifying signs of mental health issues, and connecting users with appropriate resources and professionals.

4. **Early Disease Detection:** AI algorithms can detect subtle changes in health data, potentially enabling early detection of conditions like heart disease, cancer, or neurological disorders, which could lead to timely interventions.

5. **Telemedicine and Remote Monitoring:** AI facilitates telemedicine by enabling remote consultations and monitoring, ensuring that individuals receive healthcare services regardless of their geographical location.

6. **Medication Management:** AI can assist in medication adherence by sending reminders, providing drug interaction information, and helping users understand the importance of their medications.

Challenges and Considerations

While the potential of AI in personal health management is promising, several challenges and considerations must be addressed:

1. **Data Privacy:** Collecting and storing personal health data raises significant privacy concerns. It is essential to ensure data security, obtain informed consent, and comply with regulations like HIPAA (Health Insurance Portability and Accountability Act).

2. **Accuracy and Reliability:** AI algorithms must be highly accurate and reliable to avoid false alarms or incorrect health recommendations. Continuous validation and improvement are crucial.

3. **User Education:** Users need to understand the capabilities and limitations of AI health tools. Clear communication and user education are vital to prevent overreliance or misinterpretation of AI-generated insights.

4. **Health Inequities:** Access to AI-powered health tools should be equitable to avoid exacerbating existing health disparities. Efforts should be made to make these technologies accessible to all socioeconomic groups.

5. **Ethical Considerations:** Ethical dilemmas may arise in cases where AI health tools provide life-altering recommendations or diagnoses. Transparency and accountability are essential in such situations.

The Future Outlook

The integration of AI into personal health management is expected to continue evolving. Future developments may include:

1. **Predictive Health Analytics:** AI algorithms may become even better at predicting health events, allowing for more proactive interventions.

2. **AI-Enhanced Wearables:** Wearable devices may become more sophisticated, integrating AI for real-time health monitoring and feedback.

3. **Interconnected Health Ecosystems:** AI may help create seamless connections between individuals, healthcare providers, wearable devices, electronic health records, and telehealth services.

4. **AI-Driven Preventive Care:** AI could shift the healthcare paradigm from reactive treatment to preventive care by identifying risk factors and suggesting preventive measures.

5. **AI-Powered Drug Discovery:** AI may accelerate drug discovery and development, leading to more effective treatments for various diseases.

In conclusion, AI is poised to play an increasingly significant role in personal health management. While it offers numerous benefits, addressing challenges related to data privacy, accuracy, user education, and equity is crucial to ensure that AI technologies are harnessed responsibly and ethically to improve individual health and well-being.

Section 18.1: Exploring Climate Change Information

In the face of growing environmental concerns, access to accurate and up-to-date information about climate change is essential. This section delves into the role of AI-powered search engines like Google Bard in helping individuals explore climate change information, understand its impacts, and engage in informed discussions about this critical global issue.

The Climate Change Challenge

Climate change is one of the most pressing challenges of our time. It refers to long-term shifts in global temperature and weather patterns primarily driven by human activities, including the burning of fossil fuels, deforestation, and industrial processes. The consequences of climate change are far-reaching, affecting ecosystems, weather extremes, sea levels, and human societies.

Leveraging AI-Powered Search for Climate Change Insights

AI-powered search engines like Google Bard are powerful tools for accessing climate change information and related topics. Here's how they can assist:

1. **Data Retrieval:** AI search engines can quickly retrieve a vast amount of data, including scientific studies, reports, news articles, and government publications related to climate change. This enables users to stay updated on the latest research and developments.

2. **Customized News Feeds:** Users can set up customized news feeds to receive real-time updates on climate

change news, policy changes, and environmental events, allowing them to stay informed effortlessly.

3. **Interactive Visualizations:** AI search engines can generate interactive visualizations and infographics that make complex climate data more accessible and comprehensible. These visuals can help users grasp the magnitude of the issue.

4. **Educational Resources:** Search engines can identify and recommend educational resources, including online courses, documentaries, and articles, to help users deepen their understanding of climate change.

5. **Localized Information:** AI can provide localized climate information, including regional climate trends, weather forecasts, and resources for adapting to changing conditions in specific areas.

Addressing Climate Change Misinformation

One significant challenge in the realm of climate change information is the presence of misinformation and climate denial. AI search engines can play a role in mitigating this issue by:

1. **Identifying Credible Sources:** AI algorithms can prioritize search results from authoritative and scientifically sound sources, reducing the visibility of misinformation.

2. **Fact-Checking:** Some AI tools can flag or fact-check misleading or false climate-related claims, helping users distinguish between credible information and disinformation.

3. **Promoting Scientific Consensus:** Search engines can highlight the scientific consensus on climate change, emphasizing that it is a well-established and urgent issue.

Climate Action and Awareness

AI-powered search engines are not only sources of information but also platforms for promoting climate action and awareness. Users can find resources and engage with communities dedicated to sustainability, climate activism, and environmental conservation. Furthermore, AI algorithms can recommend eco-friendly products, energy-saving tips, and ways to reduce one's carbon footprint.

The Path Forward

As climate change continues to shape our world, AI-powered search engines will remain essential tools for staying informed, combating misinformation, and fostering collective action. Their ability to provide access to accurate, timely, and localized climate information empowers individuals to make informed choices and advocate for a sustainable future. However, the responsibility also lies with users to critically evaluate information, support climate-friendly policies, and take meaningful actions to address this global challenge.

Section 18.2: Accessing Data on Sustainability Practices

In the quest for a more sustainable and environmentally friendly lifestyle, individuals and businesses seek information about sustainable practices and eco-conscious choices. AI-powered search engines like Google Bard have a significant role to play in providing access to data on sustainability, green initiatives, and eco-friendly products and services.

The Sustainability Movement

Sustainability is a multifaceted concept that encompasses environmental, social, and economic dimensions. It revolves around responsible resource use, reducing waste, minimizing carbon footprints, and promoting equity and social well-being.

As the world grapples with climate change and environmental degradation, sustainability practices have gained increasing importance.

AI-Powered Search for Sustainability Information

AI-driven search engines offer several advantages when it comes to accessing data on sustainability:

1. **Comprehensive Search:** AI algorithms can retrieve a vast amount of information related to sustainability, including articles, research papers, case studies, and reports. This allows users to explore various aspects of sustainability.

2. **Trends and Innovations:** Users can stay updated on the latest sustainability trends, innovations, and breakthroughs in renewable energy, green technology, and eco-friendly materials.

3. **Business Sustainability:** AI search engines can provide insights into how businesses are adopting sustainable practices, including information about corporate sustainability reports, green certifications, and sustainable supply chain management.

4. **Eco-Friendly Products:** Users can find information about environmentally friendly products and services, such as energy-efficient appliances, organic foods, and sustainable fashion.

5. **Sustainability Metrics:** AI tools can generate sustainability metrics and key performance indicators (KPIs) that help individuals and organizations measure their environmental impact and track progress towards sustainability goals.

Sustainable Living Resources

AI-powered search engines are valuable resources for those looking to adopt sustainable living practices:

1. **Green Building and Architecture:** Information about sustainable building materials, energy-efficient construction, and eco-friendly architectural designs can be easily accessed through AI search engines.

2. **Renewable Energy:** Users can explore options for renewable energy sources like solar, wind, and hydroelectric power. AI can provide insights into the cost-effectiveness and environmental benefits of these technologies.

3. **Sustainable Agriculture:** Information on organic farming, regenerative agriculture, and permaculture practices can assist individuals interested in sustainable food production.

4. **Waste Reduction:** AI search engines can offer tips and strategies for reducing waste, recycling effectively, and adopting a zero-waste lifestyle.

Promoting Sustainable Choices

AI algorithms can also promote sustainability by:

1. **Recommendations:** Search engines can recommend sustainable products, services, and practices based on user preferences and search history.

2. **Environmental Impact Assessment:** Some AI tools can calculate the environmental impact of various choices, such as commuting options or dietary preferences, helping users make more sustainable decisions.

3. **Community Engagement:** Users can connect with online communities, forums, and social platforms dedicated to sustainability, sharing tips, experiences, and supporting each other's sustainable journeys.

The Future of Sustainability Search

As sustainability becomes increasingly important, AI search engines will continue to evolve to meet the growing demand for sustainability-related information. Whether it's for personal lifestyle choices, business decisions, or policy advocacy, AI-powered search tools empower individuals and organizations to make informed choices that benefit both the planet and future generations. However, the ultimate success of sustainability efforts depends on the collective commitment of society to embrace and prioritize sustainable practices.

Section 18.3: Engaging with Environmental Activism

Environmental activism plays a crucial role in addressing some of the most pressing global challenges, including climate change, biodiversity loss, and environmental degradation. In recent years, digital technologies, including AI-powered search engines like Google Bard, have become powerful tools for environmental activists and organizations seeking to raise awareness, mobilize supporters, and drive positive change.

The Power of Digital Activism

Digital activism, also known as online activism or e-activism, leverages internet-based tools and platforms to promote social and environmental causes. Here are some ways in which AI-powered search engines contribute to environmental activism:

1. **Information Dissemination:** Activists use AI-driven search engines to access and share information about environmental issues, scientific research, policy developments, and more. This information can then be disseminated through social media, websites, and online forums to educate the public.

2. **Awareness Campaigns:** Search engines help activists create and optimize content for awareness campaigns. This includes articles, blog posts, infographics, and videos designed to engage and inform a broader audience about environmental challenges and potential solutions.

3. **Community Building:** AI search engines facilitate the discovery of online communities, forums, and social media groups dedicated to environmental causes. Activists can connect with like-minded individuals, share ideas, and coordinate efforts for collective action.

4. **Data Analysis:** Advanced search algorithms enable activists to analyze large datasets related to environmental issues. This data-driven approach helps identify trends, track environmental changes, and develop evidence-based advocacy strategies.

5. **Advocacy Research:** Environmental organizations use AI search engines to conduct research on policymakers, businesses, and other stakeholders. This information is valuable for targeted advocacy campaigns, lobbying efforts, and partnerships.

Mobilizing Support

AI-powered search engines play a vital role in mobilizing support for environmental causes:

1. **Petition Platforms:** Activists can discover and share online petition platforms that enable individuals to voice their concerns and demand action from governments and corporations. These platforms often use AI algorithms to match petitions with potential signatories.

2. **Fundraising Efforts:** Environmental organizations leverage search engines to reach potential donors and sponsors. By optimizing their online presence, they can attract financial support for their initiatives.

3. **Event Promotion:** Activists use search engines to promote environmental events, rallies, webinars, and conferences. These events provide opportunities for like-minded individuals to come together and strategize for change.

4. **Volunteer Recruitment:** AI algorithms can help match volunteers with environmental organizations and projects that align with their interests and skills. This streamlined approach enhances the effectiveness of volunteer efforts.

Environmental Education

AI-powered search engines are instrumental in environmental education:

1. **Online Courses:** Activists and organizations offer online courses and webinars to educate the public about environmental issues. Search engines help interested individuals find these educational resources.

2. **Scientific Insights:** Environmental researchers and scientists rely on AI-driven search engines to access scientific literature, datasets, and studies. This information aids in understanding the latest developments and findings in environmental science.

3. **Youth Engagement:** Environmental education is vital for engaging the younger generation in activism. Search engines enable youth to access age-appropriate materials, educational games, and resources that promote environmental awareness and activism.

Challenges and Ethical Considerations

While AI-powered search engines offer numerous benefits to environmental activism, they also present challenges and ethical considerations. These include issues related to misinformation, data privacy, algorithmic biases, and the carbon footprint associated with data centers. Activists and organizations must navigate these complexities while harnessing the potential of AI and search technologies for the greater good of the environment.

In conclusion, AI-powered search engines have revolutionized environmental activism by providing access to information, mobilizing support, and advancing environmental education. As the digital landscape continues to evolve, environmental activists will continue to leverage AI-driven tools to drive positive change and protect our planet for future generations.

Section 18.4: Analyzing Environmental Policies and News

Analyzing environmental policies and staying informed about the latest developments in the field is essential for individuals, organizations, and policymakers committed to addressing pressing environmental challenges. AI-powered search engines, such as Google Bard, provide valuable tools for researching and monitoring environmental policies, as well as staying updated on environmental news and trends.

Researching Environmental Policies
1. **Legislation and Regulations:** AI search engines allow users to search for specific environmental laws, regulations, and policies at local, national, and international levels. Researchers and policymakers can access official government documents and legal texts to understand the legal framework governing environmental issues.

2. **Policy Analysis:** Environmental researchers and think tanks use AI-driven search engines to conduct in-depth policy analysis. They can identify policy gaps, evaluate the effectiveness of existing measures, and recommend improvements or new policies based on their findings.

3. **Comparative Studies:** AI algorithms assist in comparing environmental policies and practices across different regions or countries. This comparative analysis helps policymakers and advocates identify successful strategies that can be adapted to address local challenges.

4. **Historical Data:** Environmental historians use search engines to access historical records and documents related to environmental policies and their evolution over time. This historical context is valuable for understanding the root causes of current environmental issues.

Monitoring Environmental News
1. **Real-Time Updates:** AI search engines provide real-time access to environmental news articles and reports from reputable sources. Users can set up alerts to receive notifications about breaking news related to environmental issues they care about.

2. **Topic-Based Aggregation:** Users can explore curated news feeds and aggregations of articles related to specific environmental topics, such as climate change, wildlife conservation, or renewable energy. This feature helps individuals stay focused on their areas of interest.

3. **Fact-Checking and Verification:** In an era of misinformation, AI search engines can assist in fact-checking and verifying news stories related to the environment. This helps prevent the spread of false or misleading information.

4. **Environmental Advocacy:** Environmental organizations use search engines to monitor news coverage of their campaigns and initiatives. This allows them to assess the impact of their advocacy efforts and adjust their strategies accordingly.

Environmental Policy Advocacy
1. **Informed Advocacy:** AI-powered search engines empower environmental advocates to stay informed

about the latest policy developments. This knowledge enables them to engage in informed discussions, write op-eds, and lobby policymakers effectively.

2. **Public Awareness:** Environmental organizations leverage search engines to raise public awareness about specific policy issues. They can create content, such as blog posts and infographics, to explain complex policies in a clear and accessible manner.

3. **Community Engagement:** Search engines help activists connect with like-minded individuals and organizations working on similar policy goals. Online forums, social media groups, and collaborative platforms facilitate discussions and coordination.

4. **Policy Impact Assessment:** Environmental advocacy groups use AI algorithms to assess the impact of environmental policies on various stakeholders, including communities, businesses, and ecosystems. This assessment informs their advocacy strategies and policy recommendations.

Ethical Considerations

While AI-powered search engines offer powerful tools for researching and monitoring environmental policies and news, ethical considerations must be taken into account. These considerations include privacy, data security, and algorithmic biases. It is essential to use AI technologies responsibly and transparently to ensure that access to environmental information benefits society without unintended consequences.

In summary, AI-powered search engines are invaluable tools for individuals, researchers, and organizations dedicated to analyzing environmental policies and staying informed about environmental news. These technologies empower users to advocate for positive policy changes, raise public awareness, and monitor the progress of environmental initiatives, contributing to a more sustainable and environmentally conscious world.

Section 18.5: Promoting Eco-Conscious Living

Promoting eco-conscious living is a vital aspect of addressing environmental challenges and fostering sustainability. AI-powered search engines, like Google Bard, can play a significant role in supporting individuals and communities in their efforts to lead environmentally responsible lifestyles. In this section, we explore how AI-driven search can contribute to eco-conscious living.

Sustainable Practices and Tips
1. **Access to Information:** AI search engines provide easy access to information on sustainable living practices. Users can find tips on reducing energy consumption, conserving water, minimizing waste, and adopting eco-friendly transportation options.

2. **DIY Guides:** Search results often include do-it-yourself (DIY) guides for eco-conscious projects. This can range from building a compost bin to creating homemade cleaning products using natural ingredients.

3. **Eco-Friendly Products:** Individuals looking to make sustainable consumer choices can search for eco-friendly products and alternatives. AI algorithms can identify products with eco-certifications and ethical sourcing.

Green Energy and Renewable Resources
1. **Solar and Wind Energy:** AI search engines help users explore renewable energy options, such as solar panels and wind turbines. Information on installation, costs, and incentives can be easily accessed.

2. **Energy Efficiency:** Users interested in reducing their carbon footprint can search for energy-efficient

appliances, insulation techniques, and home automation solutions that optimize energy usage.

3. **Green Transportation:** AI algorithms enable searches for electric vehicles (EVs), public transportation options, and carpooling services. Users can evaluate the environmental impact of their transportation choices.

Sustainable Food and Diet

1. **Local and Organic Produce:** Search engines help users locate local farmers' markets and sources of organic and sustainable food products. Users can also find information on community-supported agriculture (CSA) programs.

2. **Plant-Based Diets:** Individuals exploring plant-based diets or reducing meat consumption can access recipes, nutritional guidance, and information on the environmental benefits of such dietary choices.

3. **Food Preservation:** AI-driven search can provide information on food preservation techniques, reducing food waste, and composting organic kitchen waste.

Environmental Activism and Engagement

1. **Community Initiatives:** Search engines assist individuals in finding local environmental groups and grassroots initiatives focused on sustainability and conservation. This fosters community engagement and collaboration.

2. **Petitions and Campaigns:** Users interested in environmental advocacy can search for petitions, campaigns, and advocacy organizations addressing specific environmental issues. They can also learn about upcoming events and volunteer opportunities.

Sustainable Travel and Tourism

1. **Eco-Tourism:** AI-powered search can help travelers discover eco-friendly and sustainable tourism

destinations. Information on accommodations, activities, and responsible travel practices is readily available.

2. **Green Travel Tips:** Users can find tips on reducing the environmental impact of their travels, including eco-friendly packing, sustainable transportation options, and responsible wildlife tourism.

Education and Awareness

1. **Online Courses:** Search engines assist in locating online courses, webinars, and educational resources related to environmental conservation, sustainability, and eco-conscious living.

2. **News and Updates:** AI algorithms curate news articles and reports on environmental issues, keeping users informed about current events, climate science, and environmental policy changes.

Ethical Consumerism

1. **Product Reviews:** Users can access reviews and ratings for eco-friendly products, helping them make informed purchasing decisions aligned with their values.

2. **Comparative Analysis:** AI-driven search enables users to compare the environmental impact of different products and make choices that minimize their carbon footprint.

Community Building

1. **Online Forums:** Eco-conscious individuals can connect with like-minded individuals through online forums, discussion groups, and social media communities, fostering discussions, knowledge sharing, and mutual support.

2. **Local Sustainability Initiatives:** Users can search for local sustainability events, workshops, and initiatives, contributing to the growth of eco-conscious communities.

In conclusion, AI-powered search engines empower individuals and communities to embrace eco-conscious living by providing access to information, resources, and opportunities for sustainable practices in various aspects of life. These tools play a crucial role in promoting environmental awareness, reducing environmental impact, and fostering a collective commitment to preserving our planet for future generations.

Section 19.1: Accessibility in Different Languages and Regions

The global nature of the internet and AI-powered search engines has made it crucial to consider accessibility in different languages and regions. Google Bard, as an AI-driven search platform, aims to bridge linguistic and geographical gaps to ensure that users around the world can access information effectively. In this section, we explore the importance of language and regional accessibility in AI search engines.

Multilingual Search Capabilities
1. **Language Diversity:** One of the key strengths of AI-driven search engines is their ability to understand and process multiple languages. Google Bard supports a wide range of languages, allowing users to perform searches in their preferred language, even if it's not a widely spoken one.

2. **Translation Services:** AI algorithms facilitate language translation, enabling users to search for content in one language and receive results translated into another. This feature is invaluable for global users seeking information in a non-native language.

Cultural Relevance
1. **Localized Content:** AI search engines like Google Bard consider cultural nuances and preferences when

delivering search results. This ensures that users receive content that is contextually relevant to their region and culture.

2. **Regional News:** Users can access region-specific news and updates, allowing them to stay informed about local events, politics, and developments. This feature is particularly useful for expatriates and individuals interested in global affairs.

Global Information Access

1. **International Research:** AI search engines support academic and research endeavors by providing access to scholarly articles, papers, and publications from various countries and institutions. Researchers can explore global knowledge resources effortlessly.

2. **Cross-Cultural Learning:** Language learners benefit from AI-powered translation and language-related search features. They can practice reading and listening comprehension in multiple languages, fostering cross-cultural understanding.

Business and E-commerce

1. **Global Markets:** Businesses and e-commerce platforms can leverage AI search engines to expand their reach to international markets. Users searching for products or services can find relevant information, regardless of their geographical location.

2. **Language-Targeted Advertising:** AI algorithms enable businesses to create language-targeted advertising campaigns, reaching a broader and more diverse audience with tailored content.

Breaking Language Barriers

1. **Communication and Collaboration:** AI-driven translation tools facilitate communication and collaboration between individuals who speak different

languages. This is valuable for international business negotiations, diplomacy, and cross-border partnerships.

2. **Accessibility for Non-Native Speakers:** Non-native speakers can use AI search engines to improve their language skills by reading content in their target language. This immersive learning experience aids in language acquisition.

Bridging the Digital Divide
1. **Global Information Access:** AI search engines contribute to bridging the digital divide by providing information to regions with limited access to educational resources. This fosters knowledge sharing and empowerment in underserved communities.

2. **Preserving Indigenous Languages:** AI technologies can aid in the preservation of endangered indigenous languages by providing tools for documentation, translation, and language revival efforts.

Challenges and Considerations
1. **Accuracy and Context:** While AI translation and language processing have advanced, challenges remain in ensuring accurate translations and context preservation, especially in languages with complex nuances.

2. **Privacy and Data Security:** Collecting and processing data in multiple languages and regions raise privacy and data security concerns. It's essential to adhere to international data protection regulations.

In summary, language and regional accessibility are pivotal aspects of AI-powered search engines like Google Bard. These platforms not only break language barriers but also promote cross-cultural understanding, global information access, and inclusive communication. While challenges exist, the potential for AI-driven search to foster a more connected and informed world is significant, and continuous improvements are being made to enhance language and regional accessibility.

Section 19.2: Understanding Global Search Trends

Understanding global search trends is fundamental for AI-driven search engines like Google Bard. It enables these platforms to provide relevant and up-to-date information to users worldwide. In this section, we explore the significance of monitoring and adapting to global search trends.

Real-Time Insights
1. **Responsive Search Results:** AI-driven search engines continuously monitor global search trends and adjust search results accordingly. This ensures that users receive the most relevant and current information on popular topics.

2. **Breaking News:** Google Bard can detect breaking news and rapidly update search results, providing users with the latest developments on global events and crises.

Seasonal and Cultural Observances
1. **Festivals and Holidays:** Global search trends often align with holidays and festivals specific to different regions and cultures. AI search engines recognize these patterns, offering information related to these events, such as traditions, recipes, and celebrations.

2. **Cultural Trends:** Understanding cultural trends allows AI search engines to provide insights into the latest movies, music, fashion, and other aspects of popular culture worldwide.

Language and Content Trends
1. **Content Creation:** AI-powered platforms like Google Bard monitor content trends in multiple languages. This information helps content creators tailor their material to match what's currently in demand.

2. **Multilingual Insights:** Users searching for content in various languages benefit from AI's ability to track trending topics, making it easier to find the latest information in their preferred language.

Business and Marketing
1. **Market Research:** Businesses use global search trend data to perform market research and assess consumer interests in different regions. This information is invaluable for developing marketing strategies and product offerings.

2. **SEO and Content Strategy:** SEO professionals and digital marketers analyze global search trends to optimize their content and advertising campaigns, ensuring maximum visibility and engagement.

Educational and Research Applications
1. **Academic Research:** Researchers and academics leverage AI-driven search engines to stay updated with the latest studies and publications in their field. This is particularly important for interdisciplinary and global research projects.

2. **Language Learning:** Language learners use global search trend data to discover popular content and topics in their target language. This immersion aids in language acquisition.

Regional Insights
1. **Emerging Markets:** Global search trends provide insights into emerging markets and industries. Investors and businesses can identify opportunities in regions with increasing search interest.

2. **Social and Political Movements:** AI search engines help track social and political movements by analyzing search trends related to activism, protests, and advocacy efforts. This can be instrumental in understanding societal shifts.

Data Privacy and Ethical Considerations
1. **Privacy Protection:** While monitoring global search trends is essential, it's crucial to respect user privacy and adhere to data protection regulations when collecting and analyzing search data.

2. **Bias and Fair Representation:** AI algorithms must aim for unbiased representation in search results and avoid amplifying harmful or discriminatory trends.

In conclusion, understanding global search trends is a dynamic and essential aspect of AI-powered search engines. It enables these platforms to provide users with timely and relevant information, empowers businesses and marketers to make informed decisions, aids academics in their research, and contributes to a deeper understanding of the world's cultures and interests. However, it's vital to approach this task with sensitivity to privacy concerns and ethical considerations to ensure a fair and responsible representation of global search trends.

Section 19.3: International News and Events

International news and events play a pivotal role in shaping our understanding of the world and the issues that affect it. In this section, we delve into how AI-driven search engines like Google Bard contribute to our access to global news and events.

Global News Aggregation
1. **Comprehensive Coverage:** AI-powered search engines compile news articles from various reputable sources worldwide, offering users a comprehensive view of international events and developments.

2. **Multilingual Accessibility:** These platforms provide news articles in multiple languages, ensuring accessibility

to users globally. Language is no longer a barrier to understanding global news.

Real-Time Updates
1. **Breaking News Alerts:** Google Bard can deliver real-time alerts for breaking international news. Users can stay informed about significant events as they unfold, regardless of their location.

2. **Event Tracking:** AI algorithms can track major international events, such as elections, natural disasters, and geopolitical developments, offering detailed information and updates.

Diverse Perspectives
1. **Global Sources:** AI search engines prioritize diverse news sources, giving users access to a wide range of viewpoints and opinions on international issues. This fosters a more comprehensive understanding of complex topics.

2. **Editorial Insights:** Users can explore editorials and analyses from experts worldwide, gaining deeper insights into the nuances of international events.

Local and Regional Context
1. **Regional Relevance:** AI-driven platforms consider the user's location when presenting international news. This ensures that users receive news relevant to their region and global events that may have local implications.

2. **Local Reporting:** These platforms promote local journalism by featuring articles from regional news outlets, shedding light on global stories' local impact.

Cultural and Societal Awareness
1. **Cultural Understanding:** International news coverage helps users learn about different cultures, traditions, and societal norms. It fosters empathy and cross-cultural awareness.

2. **Societal Issues:** Global news often highlights common challenges faced by societies worldwide, such as climate change, poverty, and human rights. This encourages global solidarity and collective action.

Crisis Response and Aid
1. **Humanitarian Efforts:** Real-time updates on international crises, including natural disasters and conflicts, facilitate timely humanitarian responses and aid efforts.

2. **Fundraising and Support:** Users can access information on organizations and initiatives providing assistance to affected regions and populations, enabling them to contribute to relief efforts.

Educational Value
1. **Educational Resource:** International news is a valuable educational resource, particularly for students and researchers studying global affairs, international relations, and geopolitics.

2. **Current Events:** AI-powered search engines provide access to current events, allowing educators to incorporate real-world examples into their teaching.

Ethical Considerations
1. **Accuracy and Reliability:** While AI-driven search engines strive to provide accurate news, there is a responsibility to ensure the reliability of sources and the avoidance of misinformation.

2. **Cultural Sensitivity:** Respect for cultural nuances and responsible reporting is essential to avoid perpetuating stereotypes or misrepresenting international events.

In summary, international news and events are crucial components of AI-powered search engines. They offer users a window into the world, facilitate real-time updates on significant global developments, provide diverse perspectives, and contribute to cultural understanding and societal awareness. However, maintaining ethical reporting standards and prioritizing accuracy are essential to ensure that AI-driven platforms deliver trustworthy and responsible international news content to users around the globe.

Section 19.4: Respecting Cultural Differences in Search

Respecting cultural differences is a fundamental aspect of responsible and inclusive AI-powered search engines like Google Bard. In this section, we explore how these platforms ensure cultural sensitivity and promote diversity in search results.

Multilingual Support
1. **Language Accessibility:** AI search engines prioritize supporting multiple languages, allowing users from diverse linguistic backgrounds to access information in their preferred language.

2. **Localized Content:** These platforms understand the importance of localized content, ensuring that users receive information tailored to their region and language.

Cultural References
1. **Cultural Awareness:** AI algorithms are designed to recognize and understand cultural references, idioms, and context, ensuring that search results align with cultural norms and practices.

2. **Sensitivity to Traditions:** Search engines take into account cultural traditions and holidays, offering relevant information and resources during culturally significant times.

Inclusivity and Representation
1. **Diverse Voices:** AI-powered search engines promote diverse voices and perspectives by featuring content from creators and experts from various cultural backgrounds.

2. **Avoiding Stereotypes:** These platforms actively work to avoid perpetuating stereotypes or biases related to culture, ethnicity, or nationality in search results.

Content Filters
1. **Customizable Filters:** Users can customize content filters based on their preferences, including cultural sensitivity settings. This allows individuals to tailor their search experience to align with their values and cultural awareness.

2. **Safe Search:** AI-driven search engines incorporate safe search filters to ensure that users are protected from potentially offensive or culturally insensitive content.

Cultural Exchange
1. **Cultural Exchange Programs:** Search engines may feature information about cultural exchange programs, fostering cross-cultural interactions and promoting cultural understanding.

2. **Community Engagement:** Users can engage with online communities and forums to learn about different cultures, share experiences, and ask questions in a respectful and culturally sensitive manner.

Ethical Considerations
1. **Privacy and Consent:** Respecting cultural differences also involves adhering to privacy and consent standards. AI search engines must handle user data ethically and transparently, regardless of cultural context.

2. **Data Localization:** Some regions have specific data localization requirements. AI platforms need to comply

with these regulations while respecting cultural expectations.

In conclusion, AI-powered search engines like Google Bard are committed to respecting cultural differences and promoting inclusivity. They achieve this through multilingual support, cultural awareness, diversity representation, customizable filters, and fostering cultural exchange. However, maintaining ethical standards in data handling and respecting privacy and consent across cultures are equally vital aspects of creating a culturally sensitive and responsible AI search experience.

Section 19.5: The Global Digital Divide and Access to Information

The global digital divide refers to the gap between individuals and communities who have access to information and communication technologies (ICT) and those who do not. This divide is a critical issue in the context of AI-powered search engines like Google Bard. In this section, we will delve into the challenges posed by the digital divide and explore potential solutions to bridge this gap.

Understanding the Digital Divide

1. **Access to Hardware:** One of the primary factors contributing to the digital divide is access to computing devices like smartphones, laptops, and desktop computers. In many parts of the world, these devices are still considered a luxury.

2. **Internet Connectivity:** Reliable and affordable internet access is another crucial aspect. While urban areas in developed countries often enjoy high-speed connectivity, rural and remote regions may lack access or have limited bandwidth.

3. **Digital Literacy:** Even with access to hardware and the internet, digital literacy plays a significant role. Many people, especially in underserved communities, lack the skills to effectively use search engines and navigate online information.

Impact on Information Access
1. **Education:** The digital divide has a direct impact on educational opportunities. Students without access to online resources and search engines may lag behind in their studies.

2. **Economic Opportunities:** Access to information and online job opportunities can significantly impact economic mobility. Those without access to search engines may face limitations in their career prospects.

3. **Healthcare:** Access to health information and telemedicine services can be a matter of life and death. The digital divide may prevent people from receiving timely medical advice and treatment.

Bridging the Divide
1. **Infrastructure Development:** Governments and organizations can invest in expanding ICT infrastructure to underserved regions. This includes building better internet connectivity and providing affordable hardware.

2. **Digital Literacy Programs:** Initiatives to promote digital literacy are essential. Training programs can empower individuals with the skills needed to use AI-powered search engines effectively.

3. **Mobile Accessibility:** Mobile technology has the potential to bridge the digital divide due to its affordability and widespread use. Mobile-friendly versions of AI search engines can make information more accessible.

4. **Community Centers:** Establishing community centers with internet access and educational resources can serve as hubs for digital literacy and information dissemination.

Ethical Considerations

1. **Privacy and Data Security:** Ensuring the privacy and data security of users in underserved regions is crucial. AI-powered search engines must prioritize protecting the personal information of individuals who may be less informed about online risks.

2. **Bias and Fairness:** AI algorithms should be designed to provide fair and unbiased results, particularly for users from diverse backgrounds. Avoiding biases based on race, ethnicity, or region is essential.

In summary, the global digital divide poses significant challenges in the context of AI-powered search engines. Addressing this issue requires a multi-faceted approach that includes infrastructure development, digital literacy programs, and a focus on ethical considerations. Bridging the divide can empower underserved communities with access to information, education, and economic opportunities, ultimately contributing to a more equitable and inclusive digital future.

Chapter 20: Continuous Learning with Google Bard

Section 20.1: Keeping Up with AI and Search Engine Developments

In the rapidly evolving landscape of AI-powered search engines, continuous learning and adaptation are crucial for users to make the most of these tools. In this section, we'll explore strategies for staying informed about the latest developments in AI and search technology and how to adapt your usage of Google Bard accordingly.

The Dynamic Nature of AI and Search Engines
1. **Constant Innovation:** AI and search engines like Google Bard are subject to continuous innovation. New features, algorithms, and capabilities are regularly introduced to enhance user experiences.

2. **Changing Algorithms:** Search engine algorithms evolve to provide more accurate and relevant results. Understanding these changes is essential to optimize your search queries.

Strategies for Staying Informed
1. **Follow Official Updates:** Keep an eye on official announcements and updates from Google Bard. Subscribe to their blogs or newsletters to receive information directly from the source.

2. **Tech News and Publications:** Stay connected with tech news websites, publications, and forums. They often report on the latest advancements in AI and search technology.

3. **Online Communities:** Join online communities, discussion groups, or social media platforms related to AI and search engines. These communities provide a space

to discuss updates, share tips, and seek advice from fellow users.

4. **AI Courses and Webinars:** Participate in online courses and webinars that focus on AI, natural language processing, and search engine technologies. These courses can deepen your understanding of how these systems work.

Adapting Your Usage

1. **Experiment and Explore:** Don't hesitate to experiment with new features and search techniques offered by Google Bard. Trying out different approaches can lead to more efficient and effective searches.

2. **Customize Settings:** Review and update your Google Bard settings periodically. Tailoring preferences can help you get more relevant results.

3. **Feedback and Suggestions:** Provide feedback to Google Bard if you encounter issues or have suggestions for improvement. User feedback often plays a role in shaping future updates.

4. **Lifelong Learning:** Embrace the concept of lifelong learning. Continuously improving your search skills and understanding of AI can be personally and professionally rewarding.

Ethical Considerations

1. **Privacy Awareness:** As you adapt and explore new features, be mindful of your privacy settings and data sharing. Understand the implications of the information you share with AI-powered systems.

2. **Bias Awareness:** Stay vigilant about biases and ethical considerations in AI. Educate yourself about potential biases in search results and advocate for fairness and transparency.

In conclusion, the world of AI and search engines is dynamic, and staying informed and adaptable is key to making the most of these technologies. By following official updates, engaging with online communities, and continuously learning, you can enhance your search experiences with Google Bard while being mindful of ethical considerations.

Section 20.2: Engaging with Online Courses and Webinars

In the ever-evolving world of AI and search engines, keeping your knowledge up to date is essential to harness the full potential of tools like Google Bard. Online courses and webinars play a pivotal role in helping users stay informed and adapt to the latest advancements. In this section, we will explore the benefits of engaging with such educational resources and provide guidance on how to make the most of them.

The Role of Online Courses and Webinars

1. **Structured Learning:** Online courses and webinars offer structured and curated content that covers various aspects of AI, natural language processing, and search engine technologies. They provide a foundation for understanding these complex subjects.

2. **Expert Insights:** These educational resources are often led by experts in the field, providing valuable insights and real-world knowledge that can enhance your understanding and application of AI-powered search engines.

3. **Interactivity:** Many online courses and webinars include interactive elements such as quizzes, assignments, and Q&A sessions, fostering active learning and engagement.

Finding Relevant Courses
1. **Diverse Platforms:** Numerous platforms offer online courses and webinars on AI and related topics. Popular platforms include Coursera, edX, Udemy, and LinkedIn Learning. Explore these platforms to discover a wide range of courses.

2. **Course Selection:** Choose courses that align with your interests and goals. Whether you're a beginner looking for introductory courses or an experienced user seeking advanced knowledge, there are options available for all levels.

Tips for Maximizing Your Learning
1. **Consistency:** Allocate dedicated time for your online courses and webinars. Consistency is key to absorbing and retaining information effectively.

2. **Note-Taking:** Take notes during the sessions to jot down key concepts, tips, and ideas. This practice helps reinforce your understanding.

3. **Engage Actively:** Participate in discussions, forums, or chat groups related to the course. Sharing insights and learning from others can deepen your understanding.

4. **Apply Knowledge:** Apply what you've learned to your usage of Google Bard. Experiment with new techniques and features, and assess how they impact your search results.

5. **Continuous Enrollment:** Consider enrolling in multiple courses over time. This approach allows you to build a comprehensive knowledge base and stay updated with the latest developments.

Ethical Considerations
1. **Privacy Awareness:** Be cautious about the information you share during online courses and webinars. Protect

your personal data and consider privacy settings when interacting with others.

2. **Bias Awareness:** During your learning journey, be aware of potential biases in course content. Encourage open discussions about bias and ethical considerations in AI.

In summary, online courses and webinars are valuable resources for staying informed and adapting to the ever-changing landscape of AI and search engines. By selecting relevant courses, engaging actively, and applying your knowledge to your usage of Google Bard, you can continuously enhance your skills and make the most of AI-powered search technology. However, always remain mindful of privacy and ethical considerations throughout your learning process.

Section 20.3: Reading and Research Strategies

Effective reading and research are foundational skills for utilizing Google Bard and staying informed about the latest advancements in AI and search technology. In this section, we will delve into strategies and tips to help you become a more efficient and discerning reader and researcher in the digital age.

Navigating Information Overload

1. **Information Assessment:** The internet is flooded with information, some of which may be unreliable or outdated. It's crucial to assess the credibility and relevance of sources before relying on them for research or learning.

2. **Keyword Optimization:** When conducting online research or searching for specific topics in Google Bard, use relevant keywords and phrases to narrow down your search results. Experiment with different combinations to find the most accurate information.

Effective Reading Techniques
1. **Skim and Scan:** When faced with lengthy articles or documents, start by skimming and scanning for key points, headings, and subheadings. This helps you quickly gauge the content's relevance.

2. **Active Reading:** Engage with the material actively. Take notes, highlight important passages, and ask questions as you read. This practice enhances comprehension and retention.

3. **Summarization:** After reading, summarize the main points and takeaways in your own words. This reinforces your understanding and aids in information recall.

Online Research Best Practices
1. **Source Evaluation:** Before citing or sharing information from the web, verify the credibility of the source. Check for author credentials, publication dates, and peer-reviewed content when applicable.

2. **Diverse Sources:** Diversify your sources to gain a well-rounded perspective. Utilize academic journals, reputable news outlets, and expert blogs to gather information from various viewpoints.

3. **Critical Thinking:** Approach online content critically. Be aware of confirmation bias and seek out information that challenges your preconceptions.

Leveraging Google Bard for Research
1. **Advanced Queries:** Utilize Google Bard's advanced query capabilities to refine your research. Use operators like site:, intitle:, and filetype: to narrow down results to specific websites, titles, or file types.

2. **Topic Exploration:** If you're exploring a new topic, start with broad searches to gather general knowledge. As you delve deeper into the subject, use more specific queries to find in-depth information.

3. **Boolean Operators:** Employ Boolean operators like AND, OR, and NOT to create complex queries. These operators help you tailor your search to find precisely what you need.

4. **Time-Based Search:** When researching recent developments, use Google Bard's time-based search options to filter results by a specific time frame.

Ethical Considerations

1. **Copyright Awareness:** Respect copyright laws when using information from online sources. Cite your sources properly and, when necessary, seek permission to use copyrighted material.

2. **Plagiarism Prevention:** Avoid plagiarism by attributing ideas and content to their original creators. Use plagiarism detection tools to ensure your work is free of unoriginal content.

In conclusion, developing effective reading and research skills is essential for making the most of Google Bard and staying informed in the digital era. By assessing information critically, employing efficient reading techniques, and utilizing online research best practices, you can enhance your ability to find reliable and valuable information. Always remain mindful of ethical considerations to maintain the integrity of your research and learning endeavors.

Section 20.4: The Importance of Lifelong Learning in the Digital Age

In today's rapidly evolving digital landscape, the importance of lifelong learning cannot be overstated. With the advent of AI-powered search engines like Google Bard, staying informed and adapting to new technologies has become essential for personal and professional growth. This section explores why lifelong learning matters and how you can embrace it in the digital age.

The Changing Face of Knowledge

1. **Information Abundance:** The internet has democratized access to information, making knowledge readily available to anyone with an internet connection. However, this abundance also poses challenges in discerning reliable sources from misinformation.

2. **Evolving Technology:** Technological advancements are reshaping industries and job markets. Skills that were once valuable may become obsolete, underscoring the need for continuous learning.

Advantages of Lifelong Learning

1. **Skill Development:** Lifelong learning allows you to acquire new skills and knowledge throughout your life. This not only enhances your employability but also keeps your mind sharp and adaptable.

2. **Career Advancement:** In a competitive job market, those who invest in learning and professional development are more likely to advance in their careers and access better opportunities.

3. **Personal Growth:** Learning enriches your life by exposing you to new ideas, cultures, and perspectives. It fosters curiosity and a sense of fulfillment.

4. **Problem Solving:** Lifelong learners tend to be better problem solvers. They can apply diverse knowledge to tackle complex challenges effectively.

Embracing Lifelong Learning

1. **Set Learning Goals:** Define what you want to learn and why it's important to you. Set specific, achievable learning goals to stay motivated.

2. **Utilize Online Resources:** Take advantage of online courses, webinars, and educational platforms to access a wide range of learning materials. Google Bard can help you discover relevant resources.

3. **Join Communities:** Engage with online communities, forums, and discussion groups related to your areas of interest. Networking with like-minded individuals can provide valuable insights and support.

4. **Stay Curious:** Cultivate a curious mindset. Ask questions, seek answers, and explore topics beyond your immediate field of expertise.

5. **Time Management:** Dedicate regular time to learning. Consistency is key to making lifelong learning a habit.

6. **Reflect and Apply:** Apply what you've learned in real-life situations. Reflect on your experiences to reinforce your understanding.

Challenges and Overcoming Them

1. **Information Overload:** The sheer volume of information can be overwhelming. Practice information triage by focusing on what's most relevant to your goals.

2. **Time Constraints:** Balancing work, family, and learning can be challenging. Prioritize your learning goals and allocate time accordingly.

3. **Motivation:** Sustaining motivation for lifelong learning can be difficult. Connect your learning to your personal and professional aspirations to maintain enthusiasm.

4. **Technological Adaptation:** Embracing new technologies can be intimidating. Start with user-friendly platforms and gradually explore more advanced tools.

In conclusion, lifelong learning is a necessity in the digital age. It empowers individuals to adapt to a changing world, remain competitive in the job market, and lead fulfilling lives. With the wealth of resources available online and the support of AI-driven search engines like Google Bard, embarking on a journey of continuous learning has never been more accessible. Embrace lifelong learning as a lifelong commitment to personal and professional growth.

Section 20.5: Looking Ahead: The Evolving Landscape of AI-Powered Search

As we conclude this book, it's crucial to peer into the future and anticipate the exciting developments and challenges that lie ahead in the ever-evolving landscape of AI-powered search engines like Google Bard. The advancements in AI, natural language processing (NLP), and search technology are poised to shape our digital interactions in profound ways.

The Promise of AI-Powered Search

1. **Enhanced Personalization:** AI will continue to refine the personalization of search results, providing users with highly tailored and relevant information based on their preferences, behaviors, and context.

2. **Conversational Interfaces:** The integration of AI chatbots and virtual assistants with search engines will enable more natural and conversational interactions, allowing users to ask questions and receive answers in a human-like manner.

3. **Multimodal Search:** AI will facilitate searches across various modalities, including text, voice, images, and even augmented reality (AR). This will enable more comprehensive and immersive search experiences.

4. **Real-time Insights:** AI-powered search engines will offer real-time insights, making it possible to monitor trends, events, and emerging topics as they unfold.

5. **Accessibility:** AI-driven accessibility features will become more sophisticated, empowering individuals with disabilities to access and interact with digital content seamlessly.

Ethical Considerations
1. **Bias Mitigation:** Addressing bias in AI algorithms will remain a critical challenge. Efforts to reduce bias and promote fairness in search results will intensify.

2. **Privacy Preservation:** Striking the right balance between personalization and user privacy will be an ongoing concern. Search engines will need to implement robust privacy measures to protect user data.

3. **Transparency:** AI algorithms' decision-making processes will need to become more transparent to build trust among users. Users will demand explanations for search results and recommendations.

Collaboration and User Feedback
1. **User-Centered Development:** Search engines will increasingly involve users in the development process, soliciting feedback, and incorporating user preferences to enhance the user experience.

2. **Cross-Platform Integration:** AI-powered search will seamlessly integrate with various digital platforms and devices, offering a unified experience across devices and applications.

3. **Collaborative Learning:** Communities of users will continue to emerge, sharing insights, best practices, and collectively shaping the future of AI-powered search.

Challenges and Considerations

1. **AI Ethics:** As AI systems become more autonomous and capable, ethical dilemmas surrounding their use, accountability, and decision-making authority will intensify.

2. **Regulation and Governance:** Governments and regulatory bodies will grapple with the need for oversight and regulations to ensure AI-powered search engines adhere to ethical and legal standards.

3. **Education and Digital Literacy:** Promoting digital literacy and educating users about AI's capabilities, limitations, and potential biases will be crucial to empower individuals in their interactions with AI-powered search.

4. **Data Security:** Protecting user data from breaches and cyberattacks will remain a paramount concern. AI systems will need to implement robust security measures.

In conclusion, the future of AI-powered search is filled with possibilities and challenges. As technology continues to advance, users, developers, and policymakers must work together to harness the benefits of AI while addressing its ethical, privacy, and security implications. The journey of discovery, learning, and adaptation in the digital age will continue to be shaped by AI-powered search engines like Google Bard, making the quest for knowledge and information an exciting and dynamic one.

www.ingramcontent.com/pod-product-compliance
Lightning Source LLC
Chambersburg PA
CBHW052141220526
45471CB00004B/1475